City Limits:
Putting the Brakes
on Sprawl

MOLLY O'MEARA SHEEHAN

Jane Peterson, *Editor*

WORLDWATCH PAPER 156

June 2001

THE WORLDWATCH INSTITUTE is an independent, nonprofit environmental research organization in Washington, DC. Its mission is to foster a sustainable society in which human needs are met in ways that do not threaten the health of the natural environment or future generations. To this end, the Institute conducts interdisciplinary research on emerging global issues, the results of which are published and disseminated to decision-makers and the media.

FINANCIAL SUPPORT for the Institute is provided by the Compton Foundation, the Geraldine R. Dodge Foundation, the Ford Foundation, the Richard & Rhoda Goldman Fund, the William and Flora Hewlett Foundation, W. Alton Jones Foundation, Charles Stewart Mott Foundation, the Curtis and Edith Munson Foundation, David and Lucile Packard Foundation, John D. and Catherine T. MacArthur Foundation, Summit Foundation, Turner Foundation, U.N. Environment Programme, U.N. Population Fund, Wallace Genetic Foundation, Wallace Global Fund, Weeden Foundation, and the Winslow Foundation. The Institute also receives financial support from its Council of Sponsors members—Tom and Cathy Crain, James and Deanna Dehlsen, Roger and Vicki Sant, Robert Wallace and Raisa Scriabine, and Eckart Wintzen—and from the many other friends of Worldwatch.

THE WORLDWATCH PAPERS provide in-depth, quantitative and qualitative analysis of the major issues affecting prospects for a sustainable society. The Papers are written by members of the Worldwatch Institute research staff and reviewed by experts in the field. Regularly published in five languages, they have been used as concise and authoritative references by governments, nongovernmental organizations, and educational institutions worldwide. For a partial list of available Papers, see back pages.

The views expressed are those of the author and do not necessarily represent those of the Worldwatch Institute; of its directors, officers, or staff; or of its funding organizations.

Table of Contents

ACKNOWLEDGMENTS: Many thanks to Chris Calwell, Bill Drumheller, Walter Hook, Tanya Imola, James O'Meara (my dad), Rutherford Platt, and Lou Thompson for reviewing drafts of this paper or the *State of the World* chapter from which it grew. I am also grateful to Oscar Edmundo Diaz, Yaakov Garb, Gerhard Metschies, and Paul Steely White for their kind help with data and information. I do not have space here to list the many people who took time to explain their work to me, so their names appear in the endnotes.

Special thanks to colleagues David Roodman, for supervising this project; Jane Peterson, for enthusiastically editing the final drafts; and Michael Renner, for his comments. Thanks also to librarian Lori Brown and interns Mike Montag and David Ruppert for locating articles and books—and to Jonathan Guzman and Joseph Gravely for making sure I got all that information. I am indebted to art director Liz Doherty, who ably juggled this paper with competing demands, researchers Gary Gardner and Lisa Mastny, who reviewed the paper one last time, and to the communications team of Dick Bell, Denise Warden, Leanne Mitchell, and Niki Clark.

Lastly, heartfelt thanks to my husband, Joe Sheehan, for setting up my home office and boosting my morale.

MOLLY O'MEARA SHEEHAN is a Research Associate at the Worldwatch Institute, where she studies the role of cities and information technology in solving environmental problems. She is a contributing author of the Institute's annual books, *State of the World* and *Vital Signs*, and regularly writes for the bi-monthly *World Watch* magazine. Her last contribution to this series was Worldwatch Paper 147, *Reinventing Cities for People and the Planet.* Molly has a master's degree in Environmental Sciences from Johns Hopkins University and a bachelor's degree in Biology and Asian Studies from Williams College.

Introduction

Many mornings, in search of work to support his family, Isaac Mburu trudges eight kilometers into Nairobi's tourist district on dusty footpaths next to the city's paved roads. For three or four hours, he walks alongside speeding vehicles, squinting through brown smog. A 33-year-old father of three, Isaac lives in a neighborhood where buses never go—even if they did, he could not afford the fare. He is one of the more than 40 percent of Nairobi's residents who don't have bus fare, and one of the 94 percent who cannot buy a car. Like 55 percent of Nairobians, he inhabits a makeshift slum on the city's edge.[1]

Isaac lives in a city built for motor vehicles in a country where most people cannot afford them. Even in wealthier countries, car-centered cities deepen the disparities between rich and poor, shut out the old and young, and endanger public health. For example, though the car is the only viable means of getting from one place to another in some U.S. cities, roughly one third of the nation is too young, too old, or too poor to drive. Spread-out urban development eats up forests and farmland, paves over watersheds, and induces vehicle traffic that burns fuel and creates noise and air pollution. In Austria, France, and Switzerland, pollution kills more people than cars do: the number of premature deaths precipitated by particulate emissions from vehicles is about twice the number from traffic accidents, according to a report in *The Lancet,* a medical journal.[2]

Sprawling cities harm human and environmental health in less obvious ways as well. When people drive instead of walking or biking, they expend fewer calories. Doctors in the United States have begun to study how relying on a car to get from one place to another may foster obesity and other health risks. The greater amount of vehicle travel required in spread-out urban areas also generates carbon dioxide, a gas that warms the planet's atmosphere. Transportation is now the fastest-growing source of these climate-altering emissions.[3]

As Isaac's story suggests, spread-out cities lacking good public transportation trap people in traffic and diminish their productivity. Researchers estimate that every day, Atlanta loses more than $6 million to traffic delays, Bangkok more than $4 million. But such calculations only value hours that could have been spent working. It's harder to measure the loss to society of time that could have been used to care for one's children, build friendships, or participate in community activities. While the car is a symbol of wealth, studies suggest that the high costs of automobile dependence can actually erode economic growth. Real estate analysts in the United States have noted that denser cities that boast alternatives to the car have been better investment bets in recent years than sprawling suburban agglomerations.[4]

These sorts of problems are bound to intensify unless greater effort is made to change direction as the world continues to become more urban. Nearly half of the global population—2.85 billion people—resided in urban agglomerations in 2000, almost four times as many as in 1950. Sub-Saharan Africa, where Isaac Mburu lives, is home to the world's fastest-urbanizing countries. Demographers estimate that population growth in the cities and towns of Africa, Asia, and Latin America will account for more than 90 percent of the 2.05 billion people they expect to be added to world population between 2000 and 2030. (See Table 1.) How these cities meet the transportation needs of their citizens will affect not only billions of lives, but also world energy demand for years to come.[5]

At the same time that urbanists, environmentalists, and economists have documented the various costs of sprawl—

TABLE 1

Total Population and Share That is Urban, by World Region, 2000 and 2030

Region	2000 Population (million people)	2000 Urban Share (percent)	2030 Population (million people)	2030 Urban Share (percent)
Asia	3,683	37	4,877	53
Africa	784	38	1,406	55
Europe	729	75	691	83
Latin America	519	75	726	83
North America	310	77	372	84

Source: See endnote 5.

segregated communities, depressing landscapes, illness from polluted air and water, climate change, and economic slippage—they have also helped citizens create a vision of an urban form that would allow people greater access to jobs, schools, and stores at less cost to the environment. In countries that are already highly urbanized, new construction could be encouraged at locations easily reached by a variety of transportation means, while green space could be reserved for nature, agriculture, and recreation. Existing car-reliant suburbs could be retrofitted with bicycle paths, bus lanes, and new forms of transit. Places such as shopping malls that were designed for a single use could be rebuilt as town centers where people could both live and work.

Perhaps the greatest opportunity for pursuing the vision of people-centered cities lies in developing countries, where much new urban infrastructure will be built. Successes in places like Copenhagen, Denmark; Portland, Oregon, in the United States; and Curitiba, Brazil—three cities that have made tough decisions about transportation and urban development—are inspiring people across the planet. Satisfying the needs of walkers and bikers, centralizing new development where it can be reached by public transit, and encouraging the higher population densities needed for viable public transportation have led to cleaner air and more vibrant communities.

Yet even as this vision is transforming cities and demonstrating its superiority to the prevailing model, powerful incentives remain for people to continue building and maintaining places that cater to cars. Government institutions and policies often support car-dependent development. Transportation agencies set up to generate roads create a momentum of their own by rewarding government officials for building more roads. Zoning laws often segregate stores and other businesses from homes, making cars virtually essential for people to move from home to work or shopping. And various taxes and subsidies hide the true costs of sprawl and affect where people live and how they travel from one place to another. In Nairobi, for many years, a large fee for registering bicycles prevented poor people from buying them; Isaac Mburu, a bicycle mechanic, had his bicycle confiscated by local authorities because he could not pay the fee.

Many private companies have a vested interest in the status quo. Oil and tire companies, carmakers, road builders, and real estate developers have greatly influenced the way cities developed. Car companies, for example, spend more money than any other industry on advertising, in order to sell the idea of a car-centered life (invariably depicted on open roads) to people who may already cherish elements of this vision—a home and a car that will give them door-to-door service. Real estate developers often use money to persuade local governments to give a green light to their projects, even to flout laws designed to protect parks or other public space.

Around the world, people are tackling these institutional and political barriers, alarmed by clogged roads, dirty air, and deteriorating neighborhoods. Ideas from Copenhagen about creating safe routes for children to walk or cycle to school have been picked up and adapted by citizens' groups and local officials in the United Kingdom, the United States, and elsewhere, while elements of Curitiba's network of dedicated busways and cycle paths are being replicated in Bogotá, Lima, and other Latin American cities. And in a smart growth movement that swept across the United States in the 1990s, several states and cities borrowed ideas about metropolitan cooperation from Portland.

In helping to create visions of what they would like their cities to look like, citizens have begun to show businesses how they might collaborate to create this new urban future. As witnessed by a renaissance in light rail construction, the proliferation of privately run car-sharing networks, and the popularity of newly built neighborhoods that boast stores and offices within walking distance of homes, the companies that have responded are thriving. And so are the communities.

How Motor Vehicles Take Over Cities

With the United States leading the way, every world region has some metropolitan areas that are harmed by sprawl—or car-dependent development. The idea of sprawl and progress became intertwined long ago, and to be sure, the ranks of car owners have swollen as more people have amassed the wealth to buy vehicles. But even poor countries have built car-centric cities. Mainly, it is government decisions about transportation and housing that have created sprawl, although the dynamics have varied dramatically from place to place.

While car-dependent cities can be found all over the world, some of the world's regions harbor more than others. In studies limited to North America, Europe, Australia, and Asia, the cities sampled in the United States were the most reliant on automobiles, followed by Australia and then Canada. The cities with the highest public transit use and lowest fuel consumption were all in Europe and Asia.[6] (See Tables 2 and 3.)

This pioneering research shows that, contrary to expectations, wealth is not the main impetus toward car-centered

TABLE 2

Indicators of Automobile Dependence in Selected Cities, by World Region, 1990

Region	Private Car Use	Transportation Fuel Use	Metropolitan Population Density
	(km/person)	(megajoule/person)	(people/hectare)
United States	11,155	64,351	14.2
Australia	6,571	39,456	12.2
Canada	6,551	39,173	28.5
Europe	4,519	25,692	49.9
Asia	1,727	12,862	161.9

Sources: See endnote 6.

cities. As a group, the U.S. cities surveyed had 141 percent more car use per person than the European cities, but 15 percent *less* income per person. An even greater disparity was seen between wealthy and middle-income cities in Asia. Per capita income in Tokyo was nine times higher than that in Kuala Lumpur, Malaysia, but car use per person in Kuala Lumpur was nearly double that in rail-dense Tokyo.[7]

Car use tends to be highest in places where no other options exist. Each year, people in the United States drive almost twice as far per person as Western Europeans do. Yet U.S. citizens are not twice as wealthy, nor are they traveling twice as far with each trip. In fact, each car trip averages about the same length as one taken by a European: 13–15 kilometers (km). However, a person living in the United States generally has fewer transportation choices, so he will use a car for trips that a Western European would take by bike or train.[8]

If higher car use is not brought on by wealth or long trips, it *is* tightly linked to government transportation policies. In many countries, road networks have been expanding faster than rail systems. Transportation influences the layout of cities, so places like Atlanta and Nairobi, which have experienced major population growth at a time when govern-

TABLE 3

Commute to Work in Selected Cities, Early 1990s

City	Population (million)	Private Vehicle	Public Transit	Foot/Bicycle/ Other
			(percent)	
North America				
Atlanta	2.5	95.0	4.7	0.3
Portland	1.3	90.3	5.8	3.9
Toronto	4.3	64.6	30.1	5.3
Vancouver	1.8	81.9	12.4	5.7
Latin America				
Brasilia	1.8	45.0	53.0	2.0
Curitiba	2.2	13.6	71.8	14.6
Santiago	4.9	15.8	54.3	29.9
Bogota	6.1	8.8	74.8	16.4
Europe				
Copenhagen	1.3	43.0	25.0	32.0
Amsterdam	1.1	40.0	25.0	35.0
Paris	9.5	48.9	36.2	14.9
Zurich	0.9	36.0	39.8	24.2
Africa				
Abidjan	2.8	15.8	49.1	35.1
Nairobi	1.8	16.0	67.5	16.5
Lagos	10.3	18.5	53.8	22.4
Cairo	9.7	10.5	58.2	31.3
Asia-Pacific				
Kuala Lumpur	1.2	57.6	25.5	16.9
Jakarta	8.6	41.4	36.3	22.3
Manila	9.3	28.0	54.2	17.8
Bangkok	6.5	60.0	30.0	10.0
Hong Kong	5.8	9.1	74.0	16.9
Singapore	3.3	21.8	56.0	22.2
Tokyo	27.0	29.4	48.9	21.7
Sydney	3.6	69.3	25.2	5.5

Sources: See endnote 6.

ments were hurrying to build roads to accommodate cars, are more spread out than older urban centers.

Government housing policies have also helped to create sprawl, although the dynamics have differed from place to place. In the United States, governments coupled low-income housing in central cities with incentives for middle- and high-income people to buy houses in suburbs. Developing-country governments, on the other hand, have not subsidized suburban development in the same way the United States has, nor have they provided shelter for low-income families. Thus, whereas Atlanta has sprawling, low-density enclaves of affluent homeowners, Nairobi has sprawling, high-density settlements of destitute squatters. In each case, the city is fragmented, motor vehicles clog the roads, and people who need jobs cannot easily reach them.

The role of government policies in shaping cities is best documented in the United States, which has the longest history of car-dependent urbanization. As early as the first decade of the twentieth century, a coalition of car makers, road builders, tire manufacturers, and oil companies began forming to push Congress for a system of government-funded highways. Public disillusionment with privately run railroads, the discovery of oil in Texas, and the sense of endless space to be conquered on the American continent all contributed to the success of this effort.[9]

The National Interstate and Defense Highway System Act of 1956 launched the nation on a frenzy of highway building. Although the initial goal was to foster better roads *between* cities, the unintended result was also to build more roads *within* cities. (Today, some 36 percent of all federally aided highway miles are in urban areas.) The government poured tax revenues from gasoline into a fund dedicated to road building. The tax made users of roads help pay for them, but only partially. The taxes failed to cover the full costs of construction and maintenance, not to mention the costs from pollution or accidents. At the same time, its stable funding sheltered the Federal Highway Administration from competition with other agencies. Between 1988 and 1999, the

United States spent more than six times the amount of money on highways that it did on public transportation.[10] The lure of U.S. federal highway funds skewed the priorities of state governments. A state looking to build a highway would pay only 10 percent of the bill, while the federal government would pony up the rest. Until recently, the state of Georgia has plowed billions of dollars into highways, particularly in Atlanta's northern suburbs, while investing little in Atlanta's Metropolitan Atlanta Rapid Transit Authority. With many miles of highway and few real alternatives to the private car, Atlanta is one of the most sprawling U.S. cities.[11]

The U.S. government further boosted suburban development by underwriting both the expansion of water and sewer lines to outlying areas and the purchase of new homes there. A new government agency for home loans was created in 1938, and revamped in 1968 as a private-public enterprise, the Federal National Mortgage Association (now called Fannie Mae), to buy home loans from the banks that originate them, providing a fresh supply of money for housing. By refusing to back loans in central city neighborhoods and favoring loans in new suburban developments, the agency helped distort urban development.[12]

Most state laws allowed or even encouraged the creation of new municipalities on the edge of metropolitan areas, so new suburban towns each had their own ability to tax, zone, and establish school systems. By requiring development on large lots, these suburban towns could exclude the poor. People living in these areas could drive to the city to benefit from its cultural activities or job opportunities, but were not required to give anything back to it.[13]

Predictably, all these policies sparked a dramatic increase in car dependence. Between 1950 and 1990, the number of people living in 58 U.S. metropolitan areas analyzed by urban specialist David Rusk rose 80 percent, while the land covered by those metropolitan areas expanded 305 percent— nearly four times as much. Part of the reason that Americans now guzzle 43 percent of the world's gasoline production is to wheel around these expansive metropolises.[14]

Canada, like the United States, is a wealthy country with wide open spaces whose metropolitan areas have surged during the automobile age, but a tradition of metropolitan cooperation to link public transportation to land use planning and provide uniform services across these areas has kept sprawl in check. Canadian cities spawned suburbs in the early decades of the twentieth century, and provincial governments responded in the 1950s with an eye to the future health of the entire region by creating agencies to coordinate regional transportation, land use, and water services. Canadian metropolitan areas today have one quarter the number of kilometers in urban expressways, three times greater public transportation use, and 1.8 times greater population densities than metropolitan areas in the United States.[15]

Since the 1970s, however, Canadian provinces have expanded highways and sewers beyond the borders of regions corresponding to a single metropolitan agency, inviting U.S.-style sprawl. A shift toward political conservatism may be one reason that governments have not responded with a vigorous new expansion of metropolitan cooperation.[16]

In contrast to North America, most Western European and Japanese cities were well established before the automobile age, and most residents, treasuring their old buildings and streets, were reluctant to knock them down. People living in small, densely populated countries with long urban histories are more likely to recognize the need to cluster urban development to preserve both the character of the countryside and the fabric of cities. Moreover, nations without ample domestic supplies of oil have been more cautious in embracing the idea of a car-centered transportation system. Accordingly, governments in Western Europe and Japan have given relatively greater support to rail-based public transportation in urban areas. Western Europe has about one third of the world's urban rail systems. (See Table 4.)[17]

Today, political, economic, and demographic changes in other parts of the world are opening a window of opportunity for residents of cities to dramatically reshape them. Under central planning, governments in Central and Eastern

TABLE 4

Number of Cities with Rail Systems in Operation, by World Region, 2000

Region	Heavy Rail	Light Rail
Western Europe	29	119
Eastern Europe/Central Asia	15	166
United States and Canada	17	33
Latin America	11	6
Japan	9	20
Other Asia-Pacific	12	8
Africa	1	6

Note: Subways, elevated railways, and metros are all heavy rail, operating on rights-of-way from which all other traffic is excluded. Light rail—streetcars, tramways, or trolley cars—runs along tracks at street level that may not be separated from other traffic for long stretches.

Source: See endnote 17.

Europe sponsored urban rail and bus systems, but ran them inefficiently. Today, this region is home to some 45 percent of the world's light rail systems, but they are declining at the same time that people have gained the freedom to buy cars, and car-biased policies are being adopted. In the first half of the 1990s, the number of passengers on public trams, buses, and subways fell 8.5 percent in the Czech Republic and 13 percent in Slovakia. Between 1990 and 1996, a quarter of Hungarian towns lost their public transportation systems.[18]

Governments in Central and Eastern Europe are receiving assistance from Western Europe to improve long-distance transportation links between West and East, including major highways. In much of the industrialized world, the political coalitions that pushed for government road building began to form more than a century ago. Like poorly run transit systems in Western cities in the early part of the 1900s, those in places like Poland and the Czech Republic are no match for cash-rich Western road builders and developers, who are opening large shopping malls, or "hypermarkets," on the outskirts of towns. A developer from Long

Island, New York, where shopping malls abound, recently told a reporter that upon visiting Poland, "We flipped—we couldn't believe the opportunities.... Poland is under-retailed." In the Czech Republic, car use surged and public transit use fell as the number of suburban hypermarkets ballooned from one to 53 between 1997 and 2000. Today, the proliferation of such developments around Prague has boosted the number of hypermarkets in the Czech Republic above that in the Netherlands.[19]

Much of the developing world is urbanizing in the age of the automobile, and different kinds of sprawl are appearing. As in Central and Eastern Europe, industries that heavily influenced government transportation and urban development policies in industrial countries see huge opportunities in the developing world. According to the head of product strategy for Fiat, which plans to develop a low-cost car tailored to consumers in places like South Africa, India, and Brazil, "Over the period 1999–2007, no car market growth is predicted in the traditional industrialized countries. All the development is in emerging markets."[20]

Yet there is still time to develop cities in a way that will meet the needs of all, not only the car-driving minority. Throughout the developing world, the urban poor who cannot afford to rent or buy a home on the formal market live in squatter settlements called shantytowns, slums, or *favelas*, depending on the place. Typically located in the most inaccessible places, these neighborhoods lack city services, from water pipes and sewers to transportation. Concerns about city-wide sanitation may force officials to retrofit these areas with public utilities, but at much higher cost than if the city had set aside land for poor settlers close to major transportation corridors in the first place. Developing countries without extensive road systems still have the opportunity to develop mobility with lower dependence on the car, by setting aside rights-of-way for bicycles and buses as well as other forms of public transportation.

In the last half century, the population of Latin America has shifted from mostly rural to mostly urban, making the region the most urbanized one in the developing world. Although large cities have made important investments in bus and rail systems, they usually have not adopted complementary land use policies. For instance, in Santiago de Chile, the government added 60,000 hectares to the amount of developable land in the metropolitan area in 1979. Since then, the government has supported the construction of public housing projects far from the city's rail system and allowed low-density suburban developments along roads. With housing projects and new businesses sprouting on the city's outskirts, motorized travel has more than doubled in the last 20 years.[21]

Government policies in some parts of Asia have also begun to invite car-dependent development. To be sure, many Asian cities have a history of supporting bicycle or boat transportation. China, for instance, has provided subsidies to both bus and bicycle commuters and built separate lanes for bicycle traffic. But as urban populations and incomes have risen, cities as diverse as Calcutta and Jakarta have discouraged or even banned bicycles and other human-powered means of transportation in an effort to free up space for motor vehicles. As the roads become more dangerous for cycling, more people are taking motorcycles or cars, even for short trips. For instance, some 60 percent of very short trips in Surabaya, Indonesia, are now made by motor vehicle; in Germany, where streets are more inviting for pedestrians and cyclists, only 15 percent of such trips are by motor vehicle.[22]

Even in Africa, where the vast majority cannot afford motor vehicles, many cities elevate the needs of motorists over those of non-drivers. Africa's colonial legacy of fragmented cities is part of the reason. Europeans established new cities in previously uninhabited areas, partitioned them into racial zones, and built roads for the vehicle-driving elite. In Nairobi, for instance, the British occupied large estates served by public utilities in the city's west and northwest, while Africans were relegated to unserviced areas in the city's south and east. Today, the racial divides are blurred, but people with the most economic and political power still live in the areas served by public utilities and travel by car. Decisionmakers thus equate transportation improvements with widening roads for more motor vehicles. But remarkably simple innovations such as separate lanes and crosswalks for pedestrians would benefit more people.[23]

The Costs of Sprawl

As government policies have fostered sprawling cities, some problems with car-dependent development have become clear. Cities prosper when they can take advantage of their concentration of human talent and energy. Sprawling cities diminish that potential by segregating and dispersing people. Car-dependent development consumes land and other resources, degrading watersheds and air in the process. And car-centric cities harm economic productivity by increasing social inequities, wasting resources, and damaging the environment.

People who live in the world's most sprawling cities often need motor vehicles to participate in society in the most elementary ways: working, shopping, going to school, getting medical care. Reviewing a 1995 survey of personal transportation, the U.S. Department of Transportation found that "Americans' love affair with our cars may actually be a marriage of convenience. Contemporary land use patterns require the use of private vehicles, whether or not we love those vehicles." Half of the households in urban areas of the United States in 1990 were not within walking distance of a public transportation route. When cars are essential, being able to drive is akin to citizenship. In one survey in England, young adults were asked to choose between the right to vote in an election and the right to obtain a driving license. Some 72 percent chose the license.[24]

A lack of transportation options also creates age and gender inequities. Although car travel is the only viable means of transportation in many U.S. cities, roughly one third of Americans do not have driver's licenses. Children must rely on their parents to drive them most places, so they lose opportunities to develop the kind of independence (not to mention muscles) enjoyed by children using bikes, public transportation, and their own two feet. Only 10 percent of U.S. children aged 5–15 walk to school, a likely factor in burgeoning child obesity. Women bear a disproportionate share of the burden for ferrying children and elderly relatives immobilized by car-based transportation systems to medical appointments, for example. Even though some 60 percent of U.S. women work outside the home, women also make two thirds of the trips to take another person someplace.[25]

Sprawling cities also sharpen existing social divides, by allowing people with resources to put more space between themselves and others. Residents of suburban counties in the United States may enjoy the benefits of the entire metropolitan region, but strive to keep poor people out of their community by spurning links to region-wide public transportation and passing "snob zoning" laws that forbid the type of housing that lower-, even middle-income, people could afford. In Atlanta, although roughly 2,580 kilometers (1,600 miles) of rail and bus lines carry half a million people each weekday, these lines do not extend into three of the five counties in which the region's employment is concentrated. "It was planned that way," said Professor Robert Bullard, co-author of *Just Transportation.* "In the mid-1960s, a couple of counties basically said they didn't want public transit coming into their area because it would bring black people." Although Atlanta's suburbs are more racially integrated today, they remain segregated by income.[26]

In the United States, a downward spiral has taken hold in most sprawling metropolitan areas, where the rich and the poor live in separate municipalities, each with its own local government and budget. As people have moved to suburban areas that often exclude low-income people, inner cities have been left with a large population of people in poverty. These central city governments thus have shrinking tax revenue to address expanding social problems, and their public services suffer. As a result, the central neighborhoods become less desirable places to live, especially for those seeking schools. Myron Orfield notes that as total school enrollment in Minnesota's Twin Cities metropolitan area fell by 81,000 between 1970 and 1990, the central cities and inner suburbs closed 132 schools, while outer suburbs opened 50 new schools.[27]

When the rich succeed in isolating themselves from the poor, concentrated poverty may well drag down the economic health of the entire region. Increasingly, metropolitan areas are heralded as the basic units of the global economy. Research in the United States suggests that within these units, the fortunes of one municipality are linked to the fate of the entire metropolis. David Rusk compared U.S. cities that greatly expanded their jurisdictions to include suburban areas between 1960 and 1990 to cities whose boundaries remained fairly constant while competing suburbs grew up around them. Central cities that incorporated more suburban areas averaged an "AA" bond rating, whereas cities in the most fragmented metropolitan regions averaged only an "A" rating. Exploring the interdependence of municipalities in 74 U.S. metropolitan areas, another team of researchers concluded in their book *Regions That Work* that inequality between municipalities appears to dampen growth throughout the area: "Just like having the nicest house in an increasingly distressed neighborhood provides only a relative shield against declining property values, residing in the best gated community within a fragmented and increasingly impoverished region only hides the signs of potential and actual collapse."[28]

Car-dependent cities are more likely to trap people of all income levels in traffic, wasting everyone's time and money. Forty years ago, urban critic Lewis Mumford wrote, "What an effective network requires is the largest number of alternative modes of transportation, at varying speeds and volumes, for different functions and purposes.... By pushing all forms of traffic onto high speed motor ways, we burden them with a load guaranteed to slow down peak traffic to a crawl." Today, the Texas Transportation Institute finds that Los Angeles and Atlanta, both car-centric cities, have the two highest levels of traffic delay per person of 68 U.S. cities surveyed. This study calculates that the 4.5 billion hours of extra travel time and 6.8 billion gallons of fuel burned in traffic delays cost these 68 cities $78 billion in 1999 alone. Transportation researcher Walter Hook has found that cities such as Bangkok and Jakarta, which are less densely populated than Paris, Moscow, or Shanghai, suffer worse traffic delays because they have neither effective public transit systems nor adequate facilities for bicyclists and pedestrians.[29]

The time people spend in vehicles is time lost not only to work but also to activities that benefit personal or community health, although these losses are harder to quantify in economic terms. In the United States, public health researchers find that the share of the population that is overweight has grown in recent decades, as people's lives have become more sedentary and alternatives to driving have been reduced. Marion Nestle, a New York University professor of nutrition, and Michael Jacobson of the Center for Science in the Public Interest argue that changes in transportation and urban development are needed to halt the obesity epidemic.[30]

Car-dependent cities are more likely to trap people of all income levels in traffic, wasting everyone's time and money.

In his book *Bowling Alone*, Robert Putnam documents diminished civic engagement in U.S. society over the past several decades—and finds that urban sprawl is one likely culprit. Participation in presidential elections fell by roughly a quarter between 1960 and 1996, and the number of Roper survey respondents who said they had attended a public meeting on town or school affairs declined by 35 percent between 1974 and 1998. This disengagement occurred as metropolitan areas sprawled and the share of those driving alone to work grew from 60 percent in 1960 to 91 percent in 1995. To link these trends, Putnam cites a recent survey that finds less political involvement in homogeneous suburbs, older research showing greater public participation in less fragmented metropolises, and "time diary" studies that reveal how people spend their time. "American adults average seventy-two minutes every day behind the wheel," Putnam writes, "more than twice as much as the average parent spends with the kids."[31]

In addition to eating up more human time and motor fuel, car-centric cities require greater expenditures on transportation and other infrastructure—expenses that chip away at a region's economic potential. While the up-front cost of rail is high, cities with effective urban transit spend less on transportation over the long run. Researchers at Australia's Institute for Sustainability and Technology Policy (ISTP), led by Peter Newman and Jeffrey Kenworthy, found that auto-dependent Australian and U.S. cities spend 12–13 percent of their per capita wealth on passenger transport, whereas rail-filled cities in Europe and Asia spend considerably less (8 percent in the European cities and 5 percent in Tokyo, Hong Kong, and Singapore). Robert Cervero, a professor of planning at Berkeley, surveyed 47 U.S. cities to conclude that good accessibility between jobs and housing, and well-functioning transportation systems were key indicators of economic health.[32]

A number of studies in the United States have quantified the extra infrastructure costs required by unfocused development. Using data from these analyses, Robert Burchell found that if 25 million units of new housing in the United States were to be accommodated between 2000 and 2025 in a more space-efficient way, the nation would preserve more than 1.2 million hectares (3 million acres) of land, require 3,000 fewer new miles of state roads, and need 4.7 million fewer water and sewer "laterals." The result would be a savings of $250 billion, 75 percent in housing and development savings to developers and new property buyers.[33]

Sprawling cities also damage the environment in many ways, harming human health and ultimately affecting the economy. Slow-moving traffic in a built-up area dirties the air that many people breathe—so traffic engineers have a point when they advocate the old solution: widen roads to move vehicles more quickly into areas of low population density. What they neglect to add is that this "solution" simply extends the problem farther and that better roads invite more cars. Regions in the United States that have built new roads have fared no better at easing congestion and related air pollution than those that have not. As Michael Replogle, a transportation specialist at the U.S.-based advocacy group Environmental Defense, points out, "Adding highway capacity to solve traffic congestion is like buying larger pants to deal with your weight problem."[34]

Although a greater share of the population uses vehicles in wealthy cities, vehicles tend to be more polluting in urban centers of the developing world, where two- and three-wheeled vehicles prevail. Most of these are motor scooters and carts powered by simple but dirty "two-stroke" engines, in which much of the fuel goes unburned and is released with the exhaust. A World Bank report suggests that vehicles with such engines emit more than 10 times the amount of fine particulate matter per vehicle-kilometer as a car and only slightly less than a diesel truck.[35]

Toxic ingredients in motorcycle and car fumes cause illness, particularly among children, whose developing lungs are especially vulnerable, and among the elderly. Sulfur dioxide and particulates remain above safe levels in a number of major cities. Alone or in combination, these pollutants generate coughing and lung damage and aggravate existing respiratory problems such as asthma, which is on the rise. Daily particulate levels closely track hospital admissions and death rates.[36]

Vehicles also spew nitrogen oxides, hydrocarbons, carbon monoxide, and sometimes lead. In sunlight, nitrogen oxides and hydrocarbons react to form ozone, the main ingredient in smog, which harms human health. Wind patterns and terrain conspire to trap dirty air above sprawling cities like Santiago, which exceeded the hourly health standard for ozone 404 times in 1995, or Atlanta, which for several years has failed to meet national clean air requirements.[37]

Lives are lost not only to illnesses from vehicular pollution but also to traffic accidents. Researchers estimate that nearly a million people, mostly pedestrians, are killed on the world's roads each year. In comparing global cities, Australian researchers Newman and Kenworthy found that car-dependent cities lost proportionally more people to traffic deaths. Despite having greater measures to promote traffic safety, cities in the United States, where more people drive, had more traffic fatalities per capita than cities in developing nations in Asia.[38]

Not surprisingly, evidence from the United States suggests that cars are most likely to kill pedestrians in cities that cater primarily to motor vehicle traffic and lack sidewalks and crosswalks. In Atlanta, for instance, a rambling city where fewer than 1.5 percent of people walk to work, 185 pedestrians were killed in 1997 and 1998, making it one of the most dangerous U.S. cities to walk in.[39]

Again, the elderly and children are particularly at risk. People over 65 constitute 12 percent of the U.S. population but account for 22 percent of pedestrian deaths and 18 percent of driver deaths. Age may impair the vision and reflexes needed to drive, but car-dependent communities offer older people few alternatives to driving. As an 80-year-old Los Angeles resident recently told a reporter: "I have to have my car. I need it to get to the hospital, or see my family, or take my wife to a nice dinner. It's not a luxury. It's a big part of my life."[40]

While improvements in vehicles and fuel have helped reduce air pollution in industrial nations in the last three decades, most vehicles continue to emit carbon dioxide, a "greenhouse gas" that warms the planet's atmosphere. Worldwide, the share of carbon dioxide emissions from transportation climbed from 17 percent in 1971 to 23 percent in 1997 (see Figure 1), jacked up mainly by road traffic. Motor vehicles accounted for 58 percent of worldwide transportation carbon emissions in 1990, but their contribution grew to 73 percent by 1997.[41]

By paving over land for roads and parking lots, cities increase water problems. Much land in car-dependent cities is

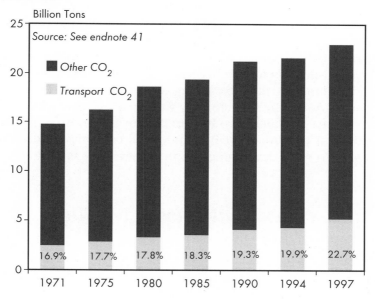

FIGURE 1

World CO₂ Emissions, Total and Transport Sector, 1971–97

Billion Tons

Source: See endnote 41

■ Other CO₂

▨ Transport CO₂

	1971	1975	1980	1985	1990	1994	1997
	16.9%	17.7%	17.8%	18.3%	19.3%	19.9%	22.7%

lost to pavement, for each car needs as much road as 4–8 bicycles, and as much parking space as 20 bicycles. Water quality and quantity both suffer in proportion to the amount of pavement that covers a watershed. Suburban development in Atlanta has impaired the health of the Chattahoochee River, which Atlanta uses as a drinking water source. Overloaded sewer systems have spewed raw sewage into the river, killing fish and making the water temporarily unsafe for swimming or fishing. Sprawling cities increase the risk of floods. Instead of seeping into the ground as it normally would, rain runs off roads and pavement into channels, where it speeds into rivers and streams, causing more severe floods than it would if plants and soil soaked up some of the deluge.[42]

Many researchers have tried to quantify the price that society pays for car-dependent transportation systems. Estimates differ because there is no single method for determining which costs to include and how to derive them. Nevertheless, numerous U.S. studies have found that motorists incur huge costs not covered by fuel taxes, vehicle taxes, or fees for road use. For example, Clifford Cobb found that the cost of driving-related air and water pollution, noise, and accidents—at $125 billion—was nearly three times greater than the $42 billion paid by drivers. A survey in the United Kingdom found that the costs of air emissions, noise, congestion, road damage, and accidents outweighed the taxes paid by drivers by three to one. Various researchers have estimated the costs of road transport not covered by drivers to be around 5 percent of GDP in industrial countries, and even higher in some developing-country cities, such as Santiago.[43]

Three Cities That Chose Livability Over Sprawl

Over the past several decades, political leaders and community activists in different parts of the world have put the brakes on car-centered urban development. Three such places are Copenhagen, Portland, and Curitiba, where political leaders have made difficult, even controversial, choices to give precedence to pedestrians and cyclists, steer new development to locations easily reached by public transportation, and maintain population densities that make public transportation and cycling possible. These decisions have helped to revitalize central city locations, improve environmental health, and make streets safer for children.

In the 1960s, just as cars were taking over the city, and public squares were being commandeered as parking lots, Copenhagen made some crucial choices. Rather than widening the roads to ease congestion, officials proposed closing streets to cars to improve conditions for pedestrians. Many people protested that Scandinavia was too cold for people to linger outside, arguing "We are Danes, not Italians!" After a lengthy debate, the city closed the main shopping street, the

Strøget, to cars in 1962. Storeowners found that the greater number of pedestrians on the street stimulated business. Over the next 11 years, adjacent streets were turned over to pedestrians. Then the focus turned to reclaiming public squares and harborsides from parked cars, and the number of parking spaces in the heart of the city was reduced by roughly 2–3 percent per year, cutting some 600 spaces between 1986 and 1996.[44]

The city also enhanced public transportation, aided by an enduring vision—the "Finger Plan." The plan, initiated in 1947, was for the urban region to develop along rail corridors extending toward smaller population centers. Copenhagen's central city was the "palm," while urban development along the five rail corridors constituted the "fingers." Green space between the fingers kept the image of a hand from turning into a paw.[45]

In addition to maintaining these rail "fingers," officials made walking and bicycling safer and easier, replacing curb-side parking with bicycle lanes and expanding the network of bicycle lanes from 180 km in 1950 to 293 km in 1995. By 1996, the city center had six times as much space devoted to pedestrians. Bicycling to and from the city center increased by some 65 percent between 1970 and 1996.[46]

In recent years, Copenhagen has built on these successes. For instance, along with other Danish cities, it has adopted a "safe routes to school" program that ensures that students have a network of safe walking and cycling paths. And to further promote transit- and cycle-friendly development, a recent government directive states that new development should occur within one kilometer of a transit station.[47]

Copenhagen's changes in the past few decades have made it far less dependent on motor vehicles. Even though the road network is bigger now than it was in 1970, the total number of kilometers driven by motor vehicles is 10 percent below the figure then. A survey of major industrial countries between 1973 and 1992 found that Denmark was the only one in which a shift from cars toward buses and rail led to a clear reduction in travel energy use and emissions. In the words of one city official, the heart of Copenhagen changed "from a car-oriented to a people-oriented" place.[48]

As a result, Copenhagen is a safe, healthy, and enjoyable place for people to live, work, and relax. Cities in the United Kingdom are now trying to emulate the Danish safe routes to school initiative. After a student exchange trip, a 14-year-old British boy remarked: "It was amazing how independent the children were in Denmark, compared to Britain. They could cycle to their basketball training, and to parties, rather than having to get taken by their parents."[49]

While people in Copenhagen were mobilizing to preserve the character of their city in the 1960s, residents of the U.S. state of Oregon were becoming concerned about the effect of suburbanization. New houses and businesses were popping up farther from downtown Portland, which was losing vitality as people moved to new opportunities in the suburbs. Nature lovers, attracted to Western Oregon by its lush greenery and woodland, and farmers whose livelihood depended on the region's rich soils, formed a coalition to protect Oregon's forests and farms from urban sprawl. In 1973, the state legislature passed a law requiring all metropolitan areas to create growth boundaries beyond which new urban development would not occur. The boundary for the greater Portland area, eventually decided on in 1980, encompassed the city of Portland and 23 neighboring towns in three counties.[50]

While the boundary was intended to protect the rural landscape, it ended up making Portlanders more aware of the urban streetscape. Under the leadership of Mayor Neil Goldschmidt, Portland began to take space from cars and give it to people. The city tore down a six-lane riverfront expressway and replaced it with a park for cyclists and walkers, and transformed a large downtown parking lot into a pedestrian plaza, Pioneer Courthouse Square, in the heart of the shopping district. Even as Portland became more consciously urban, city officials maintained a link to nature by enforcing municipal regulations to protect "view corridors" of Mount Hood, 50 miles to the east.[51]

Over the years, the city government has taken steps to promote alternatives to driving. Both building and transportation policies aim to make streets welcoming to pedestrians and cyclists. To avoid expanses of alienating blank walls, the city required ground-floor windows in new buildings, and public art to account for 1 percent of the budget of new public buildings. The city's transportation department and police department have teamed up in a "traffic-calming" program to deter speeding on city streets, especially those near schools. The city now has 240 kilometers of bikeways, and requires bicycle parking to accompany new construction. When a highway was proposed in 1975 as a link to the eastern suburbs, Portland opted instead for a light rail system called MAX (Metropolitan Area Express).[52]

Active citizens have influenced these decisions. When a highway bypass was proposed to cut through farmland to the west of Portland, two citizens' groups, 1000 Friends of Oregon and Sensible Transportation Options for People, pointed out that computer models of traffic prediction did not take into account the benefits of walkable and bikeable neighborhoods. Updating the software, these advocates showed that over 20 years, development geared toward transit, pedestrians, and cyclists would result in 18 percent less highway congestion than building a new bypass.[53]

The Portland area is now trying to apply the lessons learned in revitalizing its downtown to revamping its suburbs, which were built with office parks separated from housing developments by wide motorways. The Portland region's latest plan is to channel the bulk of future growth to nine regional centers that are to be interconnected by light rail. Up to 85 percent of new development is to take place no farther than a five-minute walk from a transit stop. The first segment of the light rail network, opened in 1990, runs east from downtown Portland; the second line, opened in 1998, traces the city's western corridor. Without the west-side rail link, planners estimate that they would have needed eight new parking garages and two extra lanes on major highways.[54]

Portland's regional government, Metro, consulted extensively with residents in formulating its latest plans. For example, Metro commissioned a survey in the early 1990s that asked citizens for their reactions to pictures of different types of streets. Most suburbanites surveyed actually did not favor the pictures of typical suburbia: wide expressways with large shopping mall blocks on either side, marooned in an asphalt sea of parking spaces, and curving residential streets fronted by two-car garages. The highest-rated residential scene was in fact a picture of a tree-lined urban street in Toronto, with 30 to 40 dwelling units per acre. Based on these sorts of surveys, Metro developed four scenarios for growth to show how the region might accommodate anticipated population increase, held 182 public meetings with citizens, made a video available through video rental stores, and sent all residents a questionnaire with maps of the different scenarios.[55]

Initial surveys uncovered double standards. For instance: "I don't like sprawl, but I don't want my neighborhood to change," or "I like transit, but I mostly drive my car." Subsequent questionnaires explicitly offered a set of trade-offs. Faced with the choice: "Should investments be made in highways or transit," only 14 percent preferred investing in roads. Only 13 percent thought that growth should occur in new areas instead of existing neighborhoods. The resulting plan employed a host of transportation and land use policies, but the vision, according to Metro's chairman Mike Burton, could still be summed up in just two sentences: "Everyone can always see Mount Hood. Every child can walk to a library."[56]

Although the suburbs within Portland's growth boundary still rely heavily on automobiles, the region's investment in transportation choices is already paying dividends. Compared to a number of more sprawling cities in the southern and western United States, Portland's streets are safer for children and pedestrians of all ages.[57]

The growing variety of transportation choices has made "car sharing" possible. Membership-based hourly car rental services took root in Europe in the 1980s. Portland's program boasts a fleet of rental cars, including a hybrid-electric sports car and a pickup truck, parked throughout the city. Members pay a $100 annual fee, reserve the car they want, walk or bike to pick it up, and receive a monthly bill for the hours used and miles driven. Steve Gutman, a participant, reports that he and his wife "share 18 vehicles with 282 people—that's 6.4 percent of one car for each of us." The Gutmans end up driving about 160 kilometers (100 miles) by car each month, much less than the typical American, and pay only $60 for transportation, a fraction of the $480 a month it costs to own and operate a relatively new car. And, says Gutman, "on any given day we have, within 10 blocks of our home, our choice of four different cars!"[58]

As in other desirable places, increased demand for housing in Portland has pushed prices up. But, contrary to critics' assertions, Portland's regional planning has likely eased the pressure. Elsewhere, suburbs put an upper limit on the number of houses per acre, effectively mandating expensive homes on large lots. Portland's Metro sets a lower limit on the number of houses and requires a mix of housing types to make housing affordable and keep a 20-year supply of buildable land within the region's boundary. Still, the target density of Portland's latest plan is less than 15 people per hectare, slightly less dense than smaller Ashland, Oregon, and far from Manhattan's 193 people per hectare. Between 1985 and 1995, lot prices increased on average 2.85 percent per year in Portland, but rose even faster in some booming places, such as Phoenix or San Diego, that lacked regional boundaries.[59]

Between the 1980s and 1990s, according to researcher Arthur Nelson, metropolitan Portland and Atlanta have seen comparable growth in population, but Portland has benefited from slower growth in vehicle traffic, reduced commuting time, cuts in air pollution and fuel use, and an increase in neighborhood quality. Moreover, both job growth and income growth were higher in Portland. (See Table 5.)[60]

Another city that opted to invest in quality public space and public transportation in the 1970s is Curitiba, Brazil. Like Portland, Curitiba started as a New World frontier town. By 1972, it was reeling from a population surge in the 1950s

TABLE 5

Changes in Portland and Atlanta Regions from mid-1980s to mid-1990s

Indicator	Portland, Oregon	Atlanta, Georgia
	(percent change)	
Population growth	+26	+32
Job growth	+43	+37
Income	+72	+60
Property tax	-29	+22
Vehicle miles traveled	+ 2	+17
Single occupant vehicle	-13	+15
Commute time	- 9	+ 1
Air pollution (ozone)	-86	+ 5
Energy consumption	- 8	+ 11
Neighborhood quality	+19	- 11

Source: See endnote 60.

and '60s that, combined with escalating automobile ownership, had brought daunting traffic problems. Under Brazil's
military dictatorship, foreign capital was flowing to large
infrastructure projects such as highways and the hasty
assembly of Brasilia, a dazzlingly modern new capital of sky-
scrapers and wide motorways that was widely touted as the
city of the future. In line with then-prevalent thinking, a
new overpass was expected to ease the Curitibans' traffic
woes. But the city's new mayor, Jaime Lerner, an architect,
believed that greater use of public transportation could ease
traffic while maintaining the character of Curitiba's streets.[61]

Lerner pointed out that the overpass would obliterate the
city's historic main street. And on the eve before demolition
was to begin, he took a highly controversial step to halt the
project, organizing engineers to block off the street to cars
and create a pedestrian mall. Bulldozer operators showed up
the next morning to find the street they were supposed to
tear up lined with flowerpots and occupied by children
painting murals.[62]

The city proceeded to manage traffic by improving public transportation, designating several main roadways radiating from the city center as axes for busways. (See Figure 2.) Zoning laws encouraged high-density buildings along these thoroughfares. Transfer stations allowed commuters on the fringes of town to switch from smaller, local buses to the express buses on the main routes.[63]

Lerner aimed not only to improve traffic but also to secure housing locations for poor families. Before the buildings along the transportation corridors were fully developed, the city bought up strategic land and set it aside for affordable housing. "These small-scale developments blend into the surrounding residential areas," writes urban analyst Jonas Rabinovitch. "They integrate rather than isolate low-income households into the economy and culture of the larger city."[64]

With the streets reconfigured, the city revamped the bus system with a series of innovations that are now world famous. Dedicated busways, extra-large buses for high-density routes, and tube-shaped shelters where passengers pay their fare in advance are adaptations from rail systems that add speed and comfort for relatively little money. In fact, the bus system cost less than one third of 1 percent of what a subway would have cost. And much of the cost has been borne by private bus companies. The city has paid only for the roads, lighting, bus stops, and staff to monitor the companies. By the mid-1990s, although Curitiba had one car for every three people, two thirds of all trips in the city were made by bus.[65]

Looking ahead, Curitiba not only steered growth toward the areas around transit lines, but also guided it away from environmentally sensitive areas. Stretches of land along rivers were put off limits to builders and made into parks, a practical option that also eliminated potential economic loss from flood damage to buildings. These re-zonings, together with other efforts to protect natural areas and build parks, increased the area of green space per person 100-fold over 20 years.[66]

The city took a host of other steps to make streets safer and easier for pedestrians and cyclists to use. What began

FIGURE 2

The Bus System in Curitiba, Brazil

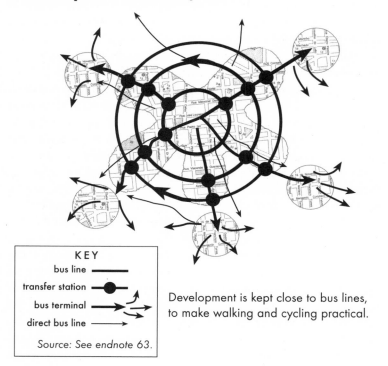

KEY
bus line ———
transfer station ●
bus terminal →
direct bus line →

Source: See endnote 63.

Development is kept close to bus lines,
to make walking and cycling practical.

with the pedestrianization of the historic main street led
to some 650 downtown blocks being set aside as pedestrian
thoroughfares. These streets connect to bus stations and
parks, which in turn connect to a 150-kilometer network of
bicycle paths.[67]

As in Copenhagen and Portland, Curitiba's transportation reforms were part of broader efforts to revitalize the central city, preserve the environment, and respond to the needs
of citizens, particularly children. In Curitiba, the city made
the needs of children central, funding municipal day-care
centers and engaging street children in city projects such as
urban gardening.[68]

When *New Yorker* writer Bill McKibben wrote in the early

1990s, "Curitiba is among the world's greatest cities," he found that many shared his view: "99 percent of Curitibans told pollsters that they were happy with their town; and 70 percent of Paulistas, residents of the mobbed megalopolis to the north, said they thought life would be better in Curitiba."[69]

The road taken by Brasilia shows what might have happened to Curitiba. The national government planned for Brasilia to have lower-density development that makes public transportation inefficient, and required residential, commercial, and industrial facilities to be separated from each other. As a result, notes an analyst for the Inter-American Development Bank, "car travel is required for even the simplest of needs" in Brasilia. Curitiba, on the other hand, by promoting development—including low-income housing—along public transportation routes and allowing residences to be located near stores, created a city in which people do not need to drive.[70]

The three cities described are by no means utopias. Outlying areas within greater Copenhagen are not as accommodating to the pedestrian or bicyclist as the center city is. Within its urban growth boundary, Portland has car-dependent suburbs and is feeling the housing demand that comes with success. Curitiba must wrestle with the problem of squatter settlements on the outskirts of town. Nonetheless, as a result of decisions to give precedence to public transportation and public space, these cities have fared better than others in many respects. Public transportation ridership has increased faster than population growth, children have better access to places they need to go, and the air is cleaner. What is more, their economies are thriving.

Linking Transportation and Land Use Policies

The stories of Copenhagen, Portland, and Curitiba illustrate how linking transportation and land use can enhance the social and economic vitality of cities. And they offer several important lessons. In many places, however, disconnected transportation investments and land use policies have spurred car-dependent development that has narrowed people's transportation choices, and created a cascade of harmful effects that were usually unforeseen.

By siting highway interchanges in a certain place, transportation planners virtually ensure that car-dependent urban development will sprout there. In the United States, this truth was not realized until after concerted highway building was under way. As head of the U.S. Bureau of Public Roads in the 1920s and the force behind the industry-supported Highway Education Board, Thomas Harris MacDonald spearheaded the coalition of car makers, road builders, tire manufacturers, and oil companies that would push Congress for a system of government-funded highways. Later, foreseeing the problems created by car-centered cities, MacDonald told the American Association of State Highway Officials in 1947 that they should work to end "the preferential use of private automobiles" and "promote the patronage of mass transit." He warned that "unless this reversal can be accomplished...the traffic problems of the larger cities may become well nigh insoluble."[71]

The transportation engineers who sited U.S. highways often made their decisions in isolation from the planners who zoned land as residential, agricultural, or rural and decided on such matters as the height of buildings and width of sidewalks. The planners themselves did not anticipate the power of the roads to transform their plans. But when engineers ran highways through cities and placed intersections nearby on land zoned for "agriculture," they ensured that pressure would build for that land to be rezoned for urban uses.[72]

This story continues to be played out in different forms around the world today. In Israel, for instance, when university professor Yaakov Garb raised concerns about the Trans-Israel highway pushing Tel Aviv to sprawl eastward, he remembers being told: "Look, we have a strong planning system. If planners want there to be development around the highway, then they will zone in development, and if they don't, then they won't." He and a colleague conducted interviews that revealed otherwise. Planners expected to be able to preserve the land around the highway for a green corridor. But a prominent developer noted, "Developers see the road as a tremendous asset, an autobahn, with potential at every entry or exit to the road. And they will do everything to realize this potential."[73]

To give people better transportation choices, governments could revise zoning laws to allow homes and stores to be intermixed, and steer new development toward places easily accessible by public transit. They could also provide safe and attractive streets for pedestrians and bicycles, while making sure that connections between cycling, rail, bus, and other forms of transportation, including paratransit, are convenient.

A common theme in the stories of Copenhagen, Portland, and Curitiba is that of people reclaiming streets and making them safer for children to walk and cycle to school. Yet sidewalks and crosswalks, a minimum requirement, are often ignored when government officials are making investment decisions. Lloyd Wright, who works on Latin American transportation projects at the U.S. Agency for International Development, says, "Very often you're in meetings where municipalities are talking about a $120 million highway interchange, and that goes through without the blink of an eye. But when we talk about a $5,000 pedestrian crossing, it's like the funds aren't there."[74]

Cities can actively promote walking and cycling by investing in bike paths and racks, slowing cars, and making streets physically appealing. Studies of Amsterdam, Bogotá, Morogoro (Tanzania), and Delhi found that these types of small investments could yield great benefits in accessibility, air quality, and traffic safety. The rewards of traffic taming have been demonstrated in the Netherlands, where a professor conceived of a street called a *woonerf*, or "living yard," in 1963. Trees and flowers, planted strategically alongside and within the street, and speed bumps to slow cars would make the woonerf more inviting than a typical street. After a number of cities tried this idea and met with success, the Dutch government adopted it nationwide. The concept spread to Germany and Austria as the *Wohnstrasse* or "livable street" in the 1970s, and then to the United Kingdom as "home zones."[75]

The most certain way to make streets safer for people and cyclists is to remove motor vehicles altogether, as Copenhagen, Portland, and Curitiba have done in some places. Many European cities ban private cars from central areas. Munich and Vienna, for instance, boast popular commercial centers that restrict motor vehicle traffic to ambulances, delivery trucks, and cars owned by local residents. A new residential neighborhood in Freiburg, Germany, bans cars entirely; about half of the residents own cars, but they keep them just outside the development. In fact, about 20 car-free communities are in various stages of development in Germany. And since 1994, more than 70 European cities have joined a Car Free Cities Network to exchange policy ideas.[76]

Enrique Peñalosa, elected in 1997 as mayor of Bogotá, Colombia, instituted a number of car-free policies. The first, *pico y placa* ("peak and plate"), takes 40 percent of private vehicles off the roads during peak morning and afternoon travel times, based on the last number on the license plate. The program reduced round-trip commuting times by up to an hour, cut accidents by 28 percent, and reduced air pollution by 10 percent. Then the city tried a bold car-free experiment in February 2000, banning private vehicles from 6:30 a.m. to 7:30 p.m. on a Thursday. Newspapers reported cleaner air, no traffic injuries or deaths, and no interruptions in the city's usual weekday functioning. Afterwards, a city-wide referendum found that nearly 90 percent of the population wanted to try it again.[77]

For a car ban to work, however, there must be other safe and speedy means of getting from one place to another, such as public transportation or cycling networks. A well-known example of a policy failure is Mexico City's "hoy no circulan" policy that banned use of certain cars on one day each week. Lacking viable transportation choices, many residents just bought an extra car—often an old, highly polluting one—to circumvent the ban. Thus a policy aimed at reducing pollution ended up worsening the problem.[78]

To avoid a similar result, Bogotá initiated a program that by 2015 will develop the city's bus service and build a subway and bicycle paths so that people can manage to restrict their private car use for three hours in the morning and three hours in the afternoon. Bogotá is densely populated enough for public transportation and cycling to work. Between 1998 and 2001, Peñalosa's administration extended the city's bicycle path network to nearly 200 km and launched a dedicated busway system. Previously, thousands of bus owners plied the streets with old, polluting buses. As in Curitiba, the city of Bogotá commissioned a fleet of cleaner, more efficient buses, and invited bus operators to bid on them. The city manages the system, while the owners of the buses make a profit on their investment. Bogotá's bus system has the added advantage of new technologies such as electronic ticketing, which makes transferring between buses easier, and satellite-based communications that boost safety by letting bus drivers call for help when needed.[79]

One type of public transportation choice that is particularly well suited to spread-out metropolitan areas is paratransit. This category embraces a range of vehicles with flexible pick-up and delivery stops—from cycle rickshaws and pedicabs to taxis and shuttle buses. In the developing world, these services employ people who need jobs and fill gaps left by regular transit routes, which rarely serve slums. The most popular type of service is a minibus or van that travels a fixed route but stops whenever a passenger wants to get on or off: Nairobi's *matatus*, Manila's jeepneys, and Buenos Aires' *colectivos*, for example. Despite the important niche paratransit fills by meeting the needs of the poor, governments often try to restrict it to make room for growing car fleets catering to the privileged.[80]

Wealthier cities are looking to computer-aided paratransit. Advances in electronic navigation, automated dispatching, and communications are making it easier for a central switchboard and computer to electronically match drivers and riders. Engineers have been applying these innovations to make "dial-a-ride" taxi services more affordable and efficient, and even design a form of personal rail transportation. A team at the University of Bristol in the United Kingdom has been developing a "personal rapid transit" system in which electrically powered four-person carriages run along a guideway. Passengers get on at any station, and their carriage stops only at their final destination. Local governments will need to reform laws governing bus and taxi routes in order to allow these new forms of public transportation to take root.[81]

The success of any type of public transportation network, from cycling to personal rapid transit, depends on having a minimum number of people within a certain area. Buses or trains only benefit the environment and the economy when lots of people use them. Researchers at Australia's ISTP have identified a critical threshold of 30 people per hectare below which public transit is not viable. The U.S. cities they have studied have, on average, 14 people per hectare, whereas the European cities have 50. A city need not be as crowded as Hong Kong's 300 people per hectare to support effective urban transit; for instance, Stockholm's transit systems work well with only 53 people per hectare. Recognizing that the success of public transportation depends on population density, places like Copenhagen and Portland are requiring new development to take place within a minimum distance from existing public transportation networks.[82]

The Netherlands has enshrined the principle of linking transportation and land use planning in its national policies. For instance, a 1990 national transport structure plan advocates urban planning as a way to solve transportation problems, noting that the government "favours compact rather than sprawling cities." The policy distinguishes accessibility, to be improved through better urban planning, from mobility—which should be constrained to reduce environmental damage. A national "ABC" policy ranks potential development sites, from the most accessible "A" locations in the "Randstad" ring of cities (including Amsterdam, Rotterdam, and Utrecht), which are well served by public transportation and bicycle paths, to relatively remote "C" locations reached only by automobile. Companies with a large number of employees and public services must be located in "A" sites.[83]

Connections to other transport networks are also crucial to making public transportation useful. One of the shortcomings of Bangkok's new Skytrain, an elevated rail system that opened in 1999, is that it lacks adequate parking for vehicles and convenient connections to bus routes. In cities such as Copenhagen and Curitiba, connections between cycling and transit make both these options more attractive. Bicycles are inconvenient for long trips and in bad weather, and buses and trains are limited to fixed routes. But bicycles and transit complement each other when people are able to carry their bikes aboard buses or trains, or to park them at stations.[84]

Buses or trains only benefit the environment and the economy when lots of people use them.

Efforts to integrate transportation and development are gaining support from architects promoting the "New Urbanism," which emphasizes the importance of urban design and regional planning in creating streets and paths that pedestrians and cyclists will want to use. These architects have drawn up local development plans that reward developers for building compact, walkable neighborhoods. A limitation of many of the projects, however, is that they have not been built around existing public transportation networks, so that residents have more attractive streets to walk on near their home but still must use a car to go most places.[85]

Many people think communications technologies will make land use planning less important, but even in the age of the Internet, when trips can be more easily replaced by "bits," there is a need for walkable neighborhoods connected by public transportation. One reason is that these technologies by themselves are not likely to reduce the total amount of transportation that occurs. Certainly, in some cases, communication will replace transportation—a teleconference, for instance, might eliminate the need for people to travel to a meeting site. But by connecting far-flung people, communications technologies have historically created the demand for new transportation. Since 1900 in France, Germany, and the United Kingdom, there has been a relatively constant ratio of transportation to communication, with around six kilometers traveled per message sent. Dutch researchers studying past expectations that telephones, fax machines, and other communications tools would substitute for transportation found that such projections failed to account for the co-existence of old and new technologies and the co-evolution of technology and society.[86]

Even as communications technology has allowed more dispersed development, it has not done away with the need for places where people can share ideas directly. "The more technology frees us from the tyranny of place and past affiliation," writes Joel Kotkin in his book on the influence of information technology on urban form, "the greater the need for individual places to make themselves more attractive." Urban centers retain their attractiveness because much of the creative work demanded by the information economy still occurs mainly in face-to-face exchange, where people live and work in close proximity.[87]

Erasing the Incentives to Sprawl

Forging a better link between transportation and land use planning is crucial for local governments wishing to stop sprawl. It is also important for local and national governments to remove incentives for cities to spread out—such as deceptive prices that favor motor vehicle-dependent development. Depending on the city or country and the type of fiscal incentives in place, a range of actions can be taken.

By subsidizing roads, sewers, and other urban infrastructure, governments make locations more desirable to build on than they would be otherwise. So by minimizing their spending on new infrastructure in outlying areas, governments can rein in sprawl. The U.S. state of Maryland approved a set of "smart growth" laws in 1997 that require the state to invest in areas that local governments have targeted for growth—generally, established communities well served by a variety of transportation modes. Since the laws were passed, the state has doubled its spending on programs that improve older neighborhoods, foster transit use, and make roads safer for pedestrians and cyclists. The share of Maryland's school construction budget devoted to improving existing schools jumped from 34 percent in 1995 to 84 percent in 1998.[88]

Local and national governments can take further steps to remove the obstacles to reusing centrally located land. Clearly, not all land within cities should be developed. As the stories of Copenhagen, Portland, and Curitiba show, parks, pedestrian plazas, and greenways along rivers are essential to improving the quality of life in a city. However, the "recycling" of old buildings, parking lots, and industrial sites has also been an important part of the story in these places.

The potential for redevelopment of substantial amounts of vacant land does exist in industrial countries, but it is even greater in places that are shifting from centrally planned to market economies. Abandoned industrial sites, or "brownfields," account for less than 10 percent of cities such as Paris or New York, but occupy 28 percent of Krakow and 45 percent of St. Petersburg.[89]

Developers are wary of building on brownfields because they do not know whether they are polluted. Local and national governments can address the concerns of developers—for instance, by changing the tax code to make the cost of cleanup deductible, as any other construction expense would be. Since U.S. states began to provide incentives for brownfield reuse less than a decade ago, some 40,000 sites have been transformed, but 450,000–600,000 sites remain.[90]

In Prague, with over 1,000 hectares of abandoned sites in the central city and developers building new suburban shopping malls, the city is becoming "Swiss-cheesed" in the words of Professor Yaakov Garb, whose Anti-Sprawl Campaign in Central and Eastern Europe assembled developers, local officials, and foreign experts on brownfield redevelopment for a seminar in April 2001. Afterwards, Garb concluded, "What we need to do is to make the brownfields not more expensive than the greenfields.... The government doesn't have to pay for all the redevelopment costs, just the difference needed to ensure those sites aren't disadvantaged."[91]

Governments can remove another incentive to sprawl by toppling barriers to credit in central locations. The U.S. government has a well-documented history of insuring home loans in ethnically homogeneous suburban neighborhoods and refusing to underwrite loans in inner city communities. (See page 51.) This bias has influenced the banks that issue loans for businesses and homes; and the resulting uneven access to credit has strongly favored investment in suburban locations over inner city neighborhoods.

The U.S. Congress took an important step toward removing the credit incentive to sprawl with the 1977 Community Reinvestment Act, which required a bank proposing to open or close a branch or merge with another company to show that it had "[met] the credit needs of its entire community, including low-and moderate-income neighborhoods...." A spate of bank mergers in the 1990s forced banks to take note of this law and, as Paul Grogan and Tony Proscio write in their book *Comeback Cities*, the effect was dramatic: "It was if the flat earth of retail banking had suddenly found its Columbus. Banks by the hundreds were planting new flags in the former terra incognita of the inner city." Total lending in low-income communities averaged $3 billion a year between 1977 and 1989; it soared to $43 billion a year by 1997.[92]

In recent years, citizens' groups have argued that homes in centrally located locations should actually be favored over suburban locations in the United States in banks' decisions about home loans. People who live in neighborhoods where they can walk, cycle, or take public transportation generally spend less on transportation and therefore have more money for housing. David Goldstein of the Natural Resources Defense Council has calculated that the average person living in an urban neighborhood in North Oakland, California, drives half as much as his counterpart in a lower-density suburb in the San Francisco Bay Area—for a transportation savings of

$250 per month, or $3,000 a year. This savings is not accounted for when banks decide how much money they will lend,
so, writes Goldstein, "a family with a modest income can be
priced out of the market for inner city locations and forced to
move to locations that not only require more driving, but
actually cost more overall," when driving expenses are added
to the mortgage payments. In the United States, several nonprofit groups have convinced Fannie Mae to lend $100 mil-
lion over two years, to allow buyers of "location-efficient"
homes in Chicago, Seattle, San Francisco, and Los Angeles to
apply their transportation savings to larger home loans.[93]

Some argue that the most widespread form of local revenue in the United States and developing countries, the property tax, could be reformed to promote development of
vacant lots within urban areas. Most property taxes merge two
distinct taxes, one on buildings and one on land. Solely taxing land could promote compact development. Buildings that
require space for elevators and stairs are more expensive to
build per square foot of usable space, so taxes on buildings fall
disproportionately on taller structures. Generally, the effect of
taxes on buildings is to raise rents, disperse construction, and
discourage urban redevelopment. A tax on land value, in contrast, is relatively benign. The worth of the land under the
building depends only on location, so, theoretically, a tax on
the land would neither deter an owner from making improvements nor promote spread-out development.[94]

Governments can also use fiscal techniques to make the
price of different transportation modes better reflect their
cost to society. Bicycling imposes few costs to society, so in
countries where a bicycle constitutes a serious investment,
governments could help to lower the barriers to purchase.
When Kenya reduced its tax on bicycles from 80 percent to
20 percent between 1986 and 1989, bicycle sales surged by
1,500 percent. Governments can also underwrite loans that
allow more people to purchase bicycles. Over the long term,
owning a bicycle saves a person money that would otherwise
be spent on public transportation and time that would otherwise be spent walking. The city of Lima launched an effort

in 1991 to increase bicycle use from 2 percent to 10 percent by 2020. Lima worked with the national government and the World Bank to open a $600,000 revolving fund that permitted people to apply for credit vouchers redeemable in bicycle shops. Between 1994 and 2000, more than 5,000 people used the credit system, with more than 4,000 of the applications coming during the last year, when the credit availability was better promoted.[95]

At the same time, the price of driving could be raised to reflect its high cost to society. This notion is gaining currency in Western Europe, where it is becoming clear, in the words of Dutch transportation analyst Jos Dings, that "trying to reduce car traffic without adjusting the price of driving is like trying to wipe water out of the cellar with the tap standing open." An increase in the "variable cost" of operating a vehicle—the cost of each trip—might be more effective in deterring excessive use than increasing the "fixed cost" through vehicle taxes, which may actually promote use because once people pay for a vehicle, they want to use it as much as possible to get their money's worth. The taxes on motor fuel, an important variable cost, are significant throughout Western Europe, so the cost of each trip is relatively high. In the United States, by contrast, the cost of buying a car has risen, while the cost of each trip has fallen. (See Figure 3.)[96]

The most direct way to increase the variable cost of driving is to raise the cost of fuel with a tax. By raising gasoline taxes, governments can generate funds for public transportation, discourage excessive driving, and encourage development of alternative fuels and vehicles. Variation in taxes account for the wide range of fuel prices worldwide. (See Table 6.) Governments could make a fuel tax hike more palatable by accompanying it with a reduction in the taxes on people's salaries or savings, or by using it to fund transportation alternatives. Experience suggests that a steady series of small price adjustments is more readily accepted than a sudden increase.[97]

Many problems caused by driving relate to the size of the vehicle or to the place or time that driving occurs. Targeted

FIGURE 3

Automobile Operating Costs, United States, 1985-98

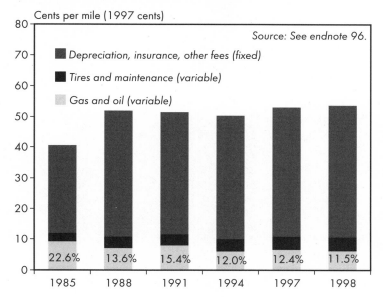

Cents per mile (1997 cents)

Source: See endnote 96.

- Depreciation, insurance, other fees (fixed)
- Tires and maintenance (variable)
- Gas and oil (variable)

Year	Percentage
1985	22.6%
1988	13.6%
1991	15.4%
1994	12.0%
1997	12.4%
1998	11.5%

incentives—charging heavy trucks for the extra wear they impose on roads, introducing fees for driving on congested roads at peak travel times, and substituting transit tickets for parking privileges—can more precisely address different concerns.

Some governments, particularly in Western Europe, have begun to adjust road-pricing policies to reflect the high cost of truck use. For instance, Iceland, New Zealand, Norway, and Sweden levy a charge on diesel trucks that rises with the weight of the truck and the distance traveled. Six nations— Belgium, Denmark, Germany, Luxembourg, the Netherlands, and Sweden—coordinate their weight-based charges across borders. Transportation analysts have proposed that the European Union adopt a unified kilometer-based charging system: all trucks would be outfitted with electronic devices hooked up to a satellite-based positioning system.[98]

Another set of policies raises the price of traveling during

TABLE 6

Gasoline Prices, Selected Countries, Fall 2000

Country	Retail Price	Tax	Tax Share of Price[1]
	(U.S. cents/liter)		(percent)
United Kingdom	113	85	76
Japan	102	55	54
France	96	67	69
Italy	95	61	64
Brazil	92	60	65
Germany	92	61	67
Spain	73	42	58
India	60	28	47
Canada	50	20	41
South Africa	50	18	36
United States	41	10	25
China	40	8	20
Russia	33	1	3
Indonesia	17	0	0

Note: Unleaded "premium" gasoline pump prices for all countries except Japan, Canada and the United States. These exceptions are unleaded "regular" gasoline pump prices. National average prices for all countries except Brazil, India, South Africa, China, Russia, and Indonesia, for which capital city prices are used. [1]"Tax Share" may not correspond perfectly to "Retail Price" and "Tax" because they are rounded.
Sources: See endnote 97.

peak times in order to reduce traffic congestion and delays. Singapore leads the world in using tolls to curb traffic. For more than 20 years, downtown-bound drivers have paid a fee that rises during rush hours; since 1998, the fee has been automatically deducted from an electronic card.[99]

Policies to raise the price of parking a car encourage people to use other types of transportation. In the United States, parking provided by employers is tax-exempt, an incentive to drive, but a relatively recent change in federal policy allows employers to give each employee up to $65 per month for public transportation. States have also changed their incentives. The state of Maryland, for instance, passed a law in 2000 that extends tax credits to nonprofit groups such as schools and hospitals if they pay for employee transit benefits or benefits equal to the cost of a parking space that the employee will not use.[100]

Governments can further lower the fixed costs of driving and raise the variable costs by providing incentives for insurance companies to offer distance-based car insurance rather than flat fees. Typically, insurance is part of the fixed cost of driving, but if insurance companies were to base their fees on the distances that people drive, then the fixed cost of driving would decline, and the variable cost would rise. The insurance company might add fees per kilometers driven to a lower baseline rate determined by conventional variables, such as age and driving record. One insurance company in the United States, Progressive Auto Insurance, already offers this type of plan.[101]

All of these actions—ceasing to subsidize infrastructure for development on "greenfields," improving access to credit for buying and building in central locations, and adjusting transportation taxes to reflect their cost to society—affect price incentives to sprawl. There are often other important "costs" to living or doing business that are higher in a central location that have nothing to do with transportation or land development. In the United States, for example, if city neighborhoods do not have good schools, families will look to the suburbs. And in places as diverse as Detroit, Nairobi, and Manila, fear of crime in the central city impels people to move to suburban neighborhoods. One could easily argue that the greatest success of places like Curitiba or Copenhagen or Portland has been in fostering central cities that are enjoyable, safe places to live.

Restructuring Government Institutions

Policies to promote urban development around public transportation and remove incentives to sprawl are far easier to recommend than to put into practice. Nations and cities face many barriers to rational development, only one of which is the structure of government bureaucracies, which tend to bias government decisions toward the status quo. At the national level, separate agencies for transportation, environment, and land use often have competing agendas. At the local level, officials of different towns within a larger metropolitan area are more likely to compete with each other than to cooperate. Further, a lack of funds may constrain local governments from taking action to coordinate transportation and land use decisions.

One way for governments to correct biases toward road building would be to reorganize bureaucracies so that decisions about transportation, environment, and regional planning are better coordinated. A 1997 study of seven Central and East European nations found that transport policies often contradicted environmental policies. And as more-established transportation ministries held more power than their environmental counterparts, transport policy priorities were able to prevail. Countries such as Denmark and the Netherlands with national agencies for spatial planning and coordinated transportation and environment policies have fared better at linking transportation and land use decisions in order to prevent sprawl. Recently, the United Kingdom took a step in this direction by forming a new integrated national agency for transportation, regional planning, and the environment.[102]

Naturally, an imbalance in the power of agencies dedicated to different modes of transportation skews policy. In the 1990s, legislation in the United States sought to bridge the divisions between road building, rail, and transit that have favored greater highway development. The landmark 1991 Intermodal Surface Transportation Equity Act (ISTEA) and its successor, the Transportation Equity Act for the 21st Century (TEA-21), allowed revenue from gasoline taxes to be used for other transportation projects. But lower-level governments have been slow to adjust to this change and backsliding has occurred. The U.S. citizens' group Surface Transportation Policy Project (STPP) has shown that between 1992 and 1997, an average of 22 percent of the federal transportation funds covered by the new legislation went to providing alternatives to driving; by 1999, the share had fallen to 17 percent.[103]

Another sort of segmentation of government encourages squabbling over transportation and land use at the metropolitan level. When new roads, rail stations, stores, industrial facilities, businesses, or houses are built in one town, transportation is affected throughout the region. A metropolitan area typically shares jobs, people, and traffic, but does not usually share an office for land use planning. By competing with each other for development, local governments tend to promote sprawl. Copenhagen, Portland, and Curitiba are all part of metropolitan regions, but these cities typically have been more powerful than the suburbs surrounding them, and higher levels of government have fostered regional cooperation.

The United States has many metropolitan areas fragmented into municipalities with different income levels. In 1950, the United States Census Bureau identified 168 metropolitan areas, containing 304 different counties; by 1990, the number of counties in those original 168 metropolitan areas had surged to 536. Until the middle of the twentieth century, developers used restrictive covenants to prevent racial minorities from buying houses in certain areas, and the Federal Housing Administration supported this practice in its decisions on insuring home loans. A 1938 manual from the agency stated: "If a neighborhood is to retain stability, it is necessary that properties shall continue to be occupied by the same social and racial classes." The Supreme Court declared racial covenants illegal in 1948, but the notion that residential developments should be homogeneous remained. The "private governments" of homeowners' associations simply replaced restrictions on race with restrictions on class, requiring more expensive, single-family homes.[104]

Among U.S. cities, Portland stands out for its high level of metropolitan cooperation. Following Oregon's 1973 law requiring growth boundaries around metropolitan areas, municipalities in the Portland region were forced to cooperate. The boundary, finally decided on in 1980, encompassed the city of Portland and 23 neighboring towns in three counties. A regional agency, Metro, was created to coordinate transportation and periodically review the need to expand the boundary. In the process of drawing the boundary, says the current head of Metro, Mike Burton, "we discovered there was a common market area, common labor pool, common transportation catchment." Subsequent laws gave greater power to Metro, making it the only directly elected regional government in the country. (The members of other regional agencies formed to coordinate transportation are typically appointed by municipalities.)[105]

Metropolitan-wide government structures are more common in Canada, which has had greater success than the United States at stemming sprawl. As suburbs grew, Canada responded by creating government agencies at the metropolitan level. Comparing Canada to the United States, researchers Tamim Raad and Jeff Kenworthy note: "In the United States, planning interventions more frequently serve local and corporate interests over regional and collective ones." On average, U.S. cities have twice as many local governments per urban dweller as Canadian cities.[106]

In Toronto, for example, the province of Ontario created an agency, Metro, in 1953 to coordinate the region's public transportation, roads, land use planning, schools, and water supply. By linking public transportation to intensive land use, Metro encouraged high levels of public transportation use. In fact, the Toronto Transit Commission has the highest ridership per capita of any metropolitan rail system in North America.[107]

However, in the decades after Metro was founded, Ontario extended highways and sewer lines outside of the Metro area, inviting sprawl. In the mid-1990s, the province proposed merging the six municipalities of Metro and joining them to the outlying municipalities, to increase the region's "global competitiveness." Suburbs worried about being dominated by the city, and vice versa, but the merger went through, creating a Greater Toronto Area (GTA). Although the GTA was granted fewer powers than Metro, it has begun to coordinate public transit, and may eventually help to stem sprawl.[108]

Metropolitan cooperation can be helped or hindered by the global trend toward giving local governments more power to provide services, including transportation. Local governments are closer to the people they represent, making them better able to respond to their needs. As mayor of Bogotá, Enrique Peñalosa was able to push through reforms because the local, rather than the national, government controls decisions about city transportation. That success is an endorsement of a decentralized system. But as economics professor Andrew Reschovsky points out, the strength of a decentralized political system must be tempered "by the realization that when urban areas are divided into a number of fiscally independent local governments, each local government has an incentive to exclude those individuals who require extra expenditures," and this fragmentation inhibits cooperation for the betterment of the region.[109]

Most metropolitan areas already have well-established local governments, so creating an entirely new level of regional government may be very difficult politically. What is needed, then, is for higher levels of government to provide incentives for local officials to cooperate. In recent years, the national government in France has been providing a monetary bonus to local governments that agree to cede some services and a portion of their tax revenue to new metropolitan or regional bodies. A similar idea would be for national governments to require metropolitan regions to develop integrated transportation and land use plans in order to receive funds for transportation projects from national tax dollars. For instance, in the United States, the ISTEA legislation requires transportation funding requests to be coordinated by a metropolitan planning organization, but these entities tend to focus narrowly on transportation. The mandate of these bodies could be expanded to include regional land use planning. Countries now in the midst of shifting power from central to local governments could build these incentives in from the beginning.[110]

Similarly, international financial and development agencies could require that regional transportation and land plans accompany requests for transportation loans. Just as the availability of money from the national budget can sway the priorities of local governments, so, too, can the policies of international banks. In developing countries, the World Bank lends over $5 billion for transportation projects, more than it does for any other sector. Between 1997 and 1999, fully 63 percent of the Bank's transportation loans went to highways, with only 15 percent to urban transport, 12 percent to rural roads, and 2 percent each to railways and waterways. A new source of transport funds for Central and East European countries is the European Union's Instrument for Structural Policies for Pre-Accession, which will cofinance with multilateral banks and national governments the extension of highways and high-speed transit from Western Europe. "By targeting improvements in long-distance links at the expense of urban transit, this money will distort transportation priorities" in Central and Eastern Europe, according to Magda Stoczkiewicz of CEE Bankwatch Network.[111]

Creating Constituencies for Change

The problems related to urban sprawl do not lack for technical solutions. Implementing these solutions, however, is a considerable political challenge. While ideas abound for revamping government agencies and policies to link transportation and land use decisions and remove incentives for sprawl, many people remain committed to the old, car-centered vision. At the same time, people around the world are starting to use the political process to put a new vision in place. Acknowledging the trade-offs needed to improve collective well-being, they are forging coalitions to convince political leaders to take action in the collective interest.

A clear vision of what people want their communities to become can be a powerful agent of change. Copenhagen's

"Finger Plan," Portland's growth boundary, and Curitiba's radial bus axes are vivid and enduring visions that all can understand. Increasingly spread through information-sharing networks, such success stories offer a sense of what is possible.

A key impetus to sprawl is the shimmering promise of individual freedom—having one's own automobile and house in a garden-like setting. In reality, once each person has an automobile and a suburban home, the dream fades. As urban critic Lewis Mumford observed, "The ultimate effect of the suburban escape in our time is, ironically, a low-grade uniform environment from which escape is impossible."[112]

The tension between individual and collective interests has long been central to environmental concerns. Although the environmental movement has helped to demonstrate that we live in an interconnected world, many people—Americans in particular—are still loath to discuss the trade-offs between individual freedom and collective well-being. In his book *How Cities Work*, Alex Marshall notes that to choose collective well-being over sprawl, Americans must recognize that some things can only be bought with political involvement and good government. "I cannot buy a healthy, friendly, and harmonious community for my child to grow up in, where people from many walks of life mingle, even if I have the wealth of Bill Gates," notes Marshall. "Our problems and our scarcities stem from scarcities of collective wealth, not individual wealth."[113]

In Portland, the regional government, Metro, made trade-offs between private and public interests clear by engaging citizens in creating a vision for the region's future. Anton Nelessen, the U.S.-based architect and professor who designed the visual preference survey used in Portland, is increasingly in demand, as other cities in the United States and elsewhere begin to engage in a public debate about what type of development citizens would like to see. Nelessen says the survey tells "mayors and city councils and planning boards, you have a license to rethink sprawl. People are always coming up to us and saying, 'no one ever asked us

what we thought about this'. They're delighted to be asked."
Peter Calthorpe and William Fulton document growing pub-
lic participation in regional planning in their book, *The
Regional City*.[114]

The region around Salt Lake City, Utah, is one place that
is thinking through future development. In 1998, a civic
group, the Coalition for Utah's Future, launched "Envision
Utah" with a series of surveys and workshops. In an exercise
called "Where Shall We Grow?" citizens analyzed how pro-
jected population growth could be accommodated on a map
that showed both the region's developed areas and natural
areas prized for beauty or recreation. The participants placed
chips on the map that represented the land area needed to
add a million people at the current average density. People
quickly realized that if they wanted to preserve parts of the
environment they cherished, then they would have to
accommodate future population growth in existing neighborhoods. Then, in 1999, the Utah state legislature approved
a measure to help local governments work together to plan
future growth.[115]

As a rule, people are only driven to envision a different
sort of urban development when they see that the current
reality is bleak. In 1998, Ted Turner, a longtime Atlanta
booster, worried that his hometown had turned into a
sprawl-plagued "hellhole." Such concerns have prompted
the search for a new vision, allowing Georgia's governor to
be elected on an anti-sprawl platform and to create a powerful new regional agency for transportation and land use.
Around the world, the economic, environmental, and social
consequences of car-dependent development are inspiring
people to work together to forge new visions.[116]

Santiago de Chile is another sprawling metropolis where
people have begun to develop a vision of what they would like
their city to be. In the early 1990s, the national government
proposed the Costanera Norte highway through downtown
Santiago, which would have paralleled the Mapocho River,
tearing up a historic district, obliterating a low-income community, separating an upper middle class neighborhood from

a scenic view of San Cristobal Hill, creating more air pollution, and making life worse for the city's pedestrians and cyclists.[117]

In 1995, some of Santiago's citizens formed a group called *Ciudad Viva* to protest the highway project. They collected petition signatures and proposed transportation reforms to government leaders. They were aided by an unlikely band of revolutionaries, the *Ciclistas Furiosos*, a group of cyclists from all walks of life—lawyers, doctors, laborers, and students—that took to the streets on the first Tuesday of every month to agitate for bicycle lanes on existing roads, new bike paths, and racks for bicycle parking. Patricio Lanfranco, a TV producer who helped to start the Ciudad Viva group, said, "We realized that the problem of traffic is a major problem, but it has a bigger context: What kind of city do we want? What kind of quality of life do we want?" Citizens finally saw results in March 2001, when the government implemented their proposal for dedicated bus lanes. Initial surveys found that the creation of the bus lanes dramatically speeded up the flow of traffic, saving commuters 25–35 minutes per trip.[118]

In Nairobi, as elsewhere in Africa, the imbalance in transportation priorities toward a minority of vehicle drivers has yet to become a political issue, but concerned citizens have begun to press for change. Jeff Maganya, who manages the East Africa Transport Program of an international non-governmental organization (NGO) called the Intermediate Technology Development Group (ITDG), notes that transportation can make or break development projects: "If schools, health centers, and water points can be built in accessible places, it cuts down on the mobility needs of most people." Working with allies in government and the civil sector, ITDG has helped bring about the cut in the luxury tax on bicycles. Maganya notes that it has been difficult to change entrenched views: "When we talked to a provincial commissioner about bicycles, he said, 'Everybody is going to the moon. Why are you giving us backward technology?'" Still, his group is reaching out to allies, from international agencies to local universities, to create a regional information-sharing network and build political momentum.[119]

Organized citizens have catalyzed coalitions to pressure governments and provided well-reasoned alternatives to existing urban development. (See list of citizens' groups in the Appendix.) While some groups have targeted local officials, others have influenced broader national and international policies. For instance, in the United States, a coalition of advocates for better transportation choices, STPP, was instrumental in drafting the ISTEA legislation that opened new funding options for alternatives to highway building. Another U.S.-based group, the Institute for Transportation and Development Policy (ITDP), has pressured the World Bank and other international institutions to rethink lending policies that contribute to sprawl. One indication of change is the World Bank's new "Urban Transport Strategy," currently in draft form. Paul Guitink, a senior transport specialist at the World Bank, points out that the new policy "moves away from private car use and towards integrating public transportation with bicycling and walking." Guitink cautions, however, that there is still much progress to be made, and expresses concern that in many projects, "if we talk about road construction and rehabilitation, we are only talking about the pavement for motorized transport, and not about providing sidewalks and bicycling facilities."[120]

In Western Europe, citizens' groups have helped awaken the public to the price incentives that influence transportation choices and contribute to sprawl. Frazer Goodwin of the European Federation for Transport and Environment (T&E) sees his organization's greatest achievement as "getting on the political agenda the debate about making the user pay the cost of transportation that is currently paid by society." Indeed, Western Europe now leads the world in using distance-based pricing for road use and shifting taxes off of income and onto fossil fuels.[121]

Even in the Netherlands, where the government has long favored coordinated transportation and land use policies, citizens are struggling to prevent car-dependent sprawl. In 1999, *Milieudefensie*, the Dutch branch of Friends of the Earth, launched an effort to persuade the government to "draw the green line" around open spaces, offering three proposals: to raise the price of sprawl through a tax on construction outside urban areas; to spur regional planning by allowing new construction only within areas designated for urban use; and to develop more parks and other green zones in and around cities. Some 200 local groups are supporting this campaign. "I think we hit something deep down inside many people, who worry...that all the open space is disappearing," says Milieudefensie's Klaas Breunissen, who is optimistic that the campaign will convince the Dutch Parliament to amend the national government's latest spatial plan.[122]

"I think we hit something deep down inside many people, who worry . . . that all the open space is disappearing."

Community groups are especially well suited to initiate efforts to reclaim streets in central cities from cars, thereby making those neighborhoods more desirable and lessening the pressure to sprawl. In the United Kingdom, citizens' groups have helped translate the Dutch woonerf into the British home zone. Lynn Sloman of Transport 2000, one of the citizens' groups, explains the appeal:

> When you go to the Netherlands and walk through these streets, you see beautifully designed public spaces with a lot of greenery, benches, tables, and play equipment.... You see very young children playing. You see neighbors sitting out eating breakfast together.... We didn't have anything like that in the UK.

Ever since Sloman's group teamed with the Children's Play Council to bring British community groups to the Netherlands to see these streets, she says, "Dozens of community groups around the country have been extremely active in lobbying for their own streets to be turned into home zones."[123]

This idea transfer from the Netherlands to the United Kingdom shows how information-sharing networks and coalitions can multiply people's efforts. Local officials around

the world formed the International Council for Local
Environmental Initiatives in 1990 to share success stories. In
Asia, the Sustainable Transport Action Network (SUSTRAN)
provides a way for citizens' groups to share ideas and information. At a United Nations meeting in New York in April
2001, ITDP brought people from SUSTRAN together with
people from Latin America and Africa who were interested in
launching similar efforts. Jeff Maganya of ITDG in Nairobi
appreciated the chance to hear from people "like the Mayor
of Bogotá, who was actually able to make a motorized-trans-
port-free place where only bicycles would come. It's almost
impossible when you haven't heard something like that to
imagine that it can happen."[124]

The stories of places like Curitiba and Portland have
already inspired many others. Lloyd Wright, of the U.S.
Agency for International Development says, "Curitiba really
started a renaissance in the way we look at buses and sustainable transportation.... If you go across Latin America,
you can see there has been a real ripple effect from Curitiba."
Similarly, as sprawl has become a political issue in recent
U.S. elections, some 36 states have debated ideas about
regional planning, from Oregon-style growth boundaries to
Maryland-style smart growth incentives. Citizens have formed
"1000 Friends" groups, based on the Oregon model, in
Maryland, Florida, Iowa, Pennsylvania, Vermont, and
Wisconsin. A Brookings Institution study documented more
than 400 ballot initiatives on managing growth that passed
in the 2000 elections, many supported by coalitions of
urban, suburban, and rural interests.[125]

To be successful, coalitions have to counter the political
power of large automotive and real estate development companies, which for many decades have used enormous advertising budgets to indoctrinate people into the idea that
sprawling development enhances freedom and prosperity. To
sell the idea of a car-centered life to the public, the automotive industry, for example, spends more money than any
other industry on advertising. (See Table 7.) In March 2001,
the *Wall Street Journal* reported that the Ford Motor compa-

TABLE 7

Automotive Sector Ranking in Advertising Spending, United States and World, 1998

Rank	Category	U.S. Ad Spending (billion dollars)	Rank	Category	World Ad Spending[1] (billion dollars)
1	Automotive	14.1	1	Automotive	9.9
2	Retail	11.6	2	Personal care	9.6
3	Movies and media	4.1	3	Food	5.2
4	Financial	3.9	4	Movies and media	2.4
5	Medicines	3.6	5	Medicines	1.6

[1]Excluding United States
Source: See endnote 126.

ny was taking advertising to a new level by underwriting a new reality TV show featuring Ford's sport utility vehicles. [126]

One way for citizens to counter this political power is to demand greater openness. Cozy relationships between industry and politicians often skew transportation and land use decisions. Citizens' groups working to stop sprawl in Central and Eastern Europe observe that city councilors may be bribed to approve a new shopping mall, or may resign after approving a project to become head of its development company. Walter Hook, director of ITDP, which has launched an anti-sprawl campaign in that region with local citizens' groups, says they are trying to unveil "the huge conflicts of interest that are promoting sprawl."[127]

Indeed, citizens' groups have a role to play in exposing how individuals and companies legally "bribe" politicians with campaign contributions. In the 2000 U.S. congressional races, industries with a stake in transportation and land use decisions contributed some $218 million to political parties and candidates—17 percent of the total spent by major industry groups—which doesn't count what they spend on lobbying. Such groups often influence the way that lawmakers vote. For example, the auto industry successfully lobbied the U.S. Congress to halt increases in fuel efficiency standards in the 1990s.[128]

Coalitions for a new type of urban development need to show businesses how they can gain. Obviously, bicycle and rail manufacturers will see a role for themselves in a vision of walkable neighborhoods connected by cycle paths and public transportation. Indeed, a resurgence of interest in light rail in Western Europe has reversed a decades-long decline in this form of transport, and light rail riders are the fastest-growing segment of public transit users in the United States. The number of Americans riding public transportation in general has risen for five straight years. Automotive, energy, and real estate companies also need to be shown how they could re-position themselves.[129]

Automotive companies, for example, could, over time, become sellers of transportation services. With a variety of transportation choices available, consumers would be able to choose the best mode for each trip. If cycling and transit were flourishing, and the price of driving were to reflect its full costs, then people would be more likely to choose cars only when they really made sense. A huge, fuel-guzzling sport utility vehicle would lose its appeal for a daily urban commute. Auto companies could woo consumers with the exact type of rental car they needed for a given trip: a small, electric car for city use, a sporty convertible for a romantic weekend getaway, a station wagon for a family vacation, a sport utility vehicle for a once-a-year trip to the mountains, or a truck for moving furniture.

This idea is not so farfetched. Privately run car-sharing networks, popular in Europe and recently introduced to a few North American cities, give people easy access to a car without the high costs of owning or the hassles of renting. Members are more likely to use a car only for the trips where it has a significant advantage over other modes. Even the chairman of Ford has acknowledged the potential of these services, stating: "The idea that everybody must own an individual car will also vanish in the long run. The manufacturers could offer the cars to the drivers on demand for pay. The day will come when the notion of car ownership becomes antiquated."[130]

At the same time, real estate developers stand to benefit by tapping a market of people who do not want to live in places where, in the words of essayist E.B. White, "Everything in life is somewhere else, and you get there in a car." In the United States, some 150 communities designed on New Urbanist principles, where people can walk or cycle to many locations, are at some stage of development, and selling at a premium compared to conventional sprawl.[131]

Perhaps the biggest opportunities for communities to engage the business community in their vision for the future exists in Latin America, Asia, Africa, and Central and Eastern Europe, where people are making major decisions today about investment in transportation and development that will affect people's lives for decades to come. Patricio Lanfranco, of Ciudad Viva in Santiago, recognizes this. In a city where only 20 percent of people can afford to commute by car, Ciudad Viva sees a great opportunity for the government to claim streets for a bus network like Curitiba's. "What we are saying to business people," says Lanfranco, "is to get out of the business of private cars. What you have to do is make or sell mass transportation vehicles, and we are going to ensure you access to at least 80 percent of the market. It's a great deal, isn't it?"[132]

There is a similar window of opportunity in Central and Eastern Europe. Magda Stoczkiewicz of Central and Eastern Europe Bankwatch says, "In many towns we still have very good train and bus systems. It's still not too late to stop car-dependent development." An anti-sprawl campaign in this region is trying to increase the bargaining power of cities in Czechoslovakia, Hungary, and Poland to attract developers to build the types of things communities would like to see within their cities. This group would like to see local officials responsible for brownfield sites work with communities to develop a vision for the future use of the land. After clearly articulating these aspirations, officials would let developers offer their proposals.[133]

The importance of engaging businesses and appealing to

consumers cannot be overstated. In his book *Getting There*, Stephen Goddard details the many ways in which both rail and road industries manipulated public opinion to influence U.S. policymakers. Road supporters won by forging coalitions in the first decades of the twentieth century that "put government engineers and bureaucrats in touch regularly with auto and rubber executives and engineering professors." The road interests also prevailed because they were able to embed in the American psyche the idea that the rails were the transport of the past, run by greedy corporate interests, whereas the roads were depicted as the more democratic and technologically superior transport of the future.[134]

Stories such as the successes of Curitiba or Copenhagen would be even more powerful if they could convince businesses of new investment opportunities and reach a broader audience of voters and consumers. As Enrique Peñalosa of Bogotá says, "We get a lot of television from the United States, a lot of car races and highways. But we don't get many TV shows from Copenhagen. People would never think that an advanced country would have people riding around on bikes." In April 2001, the city of Bremen, Germany, gave the first awards in a new program to highlight examples worldwide of businesses and municipalities working together to promote sustainable development.[135]

With many of the world's cities increasingly dominated by highways and motor vehicles, their harsh impact on social harmony, human health, and the environment are clear. Car-centric development diminishes human and economic potential. Both markets and constituencies exist for cleaner, walkable neighborhoods, efficient transit, and healthier regions. In the United Kingdom, surveys by the Department of the Environment found that the percentage of people interviewed who were "very worried" about traffic-related smog increased from 23 percent in 1986 to 40 percent in 1993. Surveys by the Pew Center for Civic Journalism in 1999 found urban sprawl to be the top local concern of U.S. residents.[136]

The United States, which created the model of urban sprawl, now has the longest history of dealing with the problems it has spawned. President Dwight D. Eisenhower, who signed the 1956 law establishing the national interstate system, may have been one of the first to recognize the problems. Apparently, Eisenhower had believed the highways would go around cities, not through them (when, in fact, local officials had jumped at the chance to get federal funds for a public works project). On his way out of Washington, DC, to Camp David, Maryland, in 1959, Eisenhower saw bulldozers cutting a swath of land through the northwest part of the city and was shocked to learn that the highway project was part of his interstate system. By the end of his term, the president regretfully concluded there was nothing he could do to reverse the situation, remarking on the wastefulness of motorists "driving into the central area and taking all the space required to park the cars."[137]

Today, as many more people understand that sprawling cities that cater to the automobile are the result of government choices to foster road building, car infrastructure, and spread out development, they realize that they could pressure their leaders to choose a different future. Cities could be made more socially cohesive, environmentally healthy, and economically vibrant with integrated networks for bicycles, bus, rail, and new types of transit. As excitement builds in Bogotá over its new bus system and bike paths, former Mayor Peñalosa reflects: "We are still miles away from where we would like to be, but there is a change in mentality that is incredible. When you have people talking about how they would like to live, and they think that they have the power to choose, this is a very important change."[138]

Appendix

Some Groups that Support Transportation Choices for Livable Cities

Networks of Citizens or Local Authorities

Center for Neighborhood Technology
2125 W. North Ave.
Chicago, IL 60647 USA
tel.: (773) 278-4800; fax: (773) 278-3840
website: www.cnt.org
Created to foster self-sufficient neighborhoods in Chicago, but now seeks to link economic development with ecological improvement in communities nationwide.

CityNet
International Organization Centre, 5F
Pacifico-Yokohama, Minato Mirai, Nishi-ku
Yokohama 220-0012 Japan
tel.: 81 45 223 2161; fax: 81 45 223 2162
e-mail: info@citynet-ap.org
website: www.citynet-ap.org
Network of local governments, NGOs, and research institutes in the Asia-Pacific region.

Congress for the New Urbanism
Hearst Building
5 Third St., Suite 500A
San Francisco, CA 94103 USA
tel.: (415) 495-2255; fax: (415) 495-1731
e-mail: cnuinfo@cnu.org
website: www.cnu.org
Works with architects and planners to promote regional planning, walkable neighborhoods, and attractive public spaces.

European Federation for Transport and the Environment
34 boulevard de Waterloo
B-1000 Brussels, Belgium
tel.: 2 2 502 99 09; fax: 32 2 502 99 08
e-mail: info@t-e.nu
website: www.t-e.nu/index.htm

Umbrella group of NGOs that proposes transport policies to the European Union.

Institute for Transportation and Development Policy (ITDP)
115 W. 30th St., Suite 1205
New York, NY 10001 USA
tel.: (212) 629-8001; fax: (212) 629-8033
e-mail: mobility@igc.org
website: www.itdp.org
Works with local groups in Eastern Europe, Asia, Africa, and Latin America toward greener and more equitable transportation and development. Has launched an "Anti-sprawl Campaign" in Central and Eastern Europe.

International Council for Local Environmental Initiatives (ICLEI)
City Hall East Tower 8th Floor
Toronto, Ontario M5H 2N2 Canada
tel.: (416) 392-1462; fax: (416) 392-1478
e-mail: iclei@iclei.org
website: www.iclei.org
An association of local governments, ICLEI helps cities share success stories.

1000 Friends of Oregon
534 SW Third Ave., Suite 300
Portland, OR 97204 USA
tel.: (503) 497-1000; fax: (503) 223-0073
e-mail: info@friends.org
website: www.friends.org
Researches land use policies, educates citizens, and advocates responsible planning in Oregon. Website links to similar U.S. groups.

Sustainable Transport Action Network for Asia and the Pacific (SUSTRAN)
c/o Pelangi Indonesia, Jl. Danau Tondano No. A-4
Jakarta 10210 Indonesia
tel.: 62 21 573 5020, 571 9360; fax: 62 21 573 2503
e-mail: kuki@pelangi.or.id or bsantono@pelangi.or.id
website: www.geocities.com/sustrannet
NGO network that distributes an electronic newsletter on efforts to improve transportation in the Asia-Pacific region.

Smart Growth Network
International City/County Management Association
777 North Capitol St., NE, Suite 500
Washington, DC 20002-4201 USA
tel.: (202) 962-3591; fax: (202) 962-3500
e-mail: info@smartgrowth.org
website: www.smartgrowth.org
Sponsored by the U.S. Environmental Protection Agency to share
information on transportation and land use planning.

Surface Transportation Policy Project (STPP)
1100 17th St., NW, 10th Floor
Washington, DC 20036 USA
tel.: (202) 466-2636; fax: (202) 466-2247
e-mail: stpp@transact.org
website: www.transact.org
Advocates transportation policies to protect neighborhoods, provide better travel choices, and promote social equity. Keeps a list
of U.S. groups working on these issues.

Research Institutes and Journals

Center on Urban and Metropolitan Policy
Brookings Institution
1775 Massachusetts Ave., NW
Washington, DC 20036 USA
tel.: (202) 797-6139; fax: (202) 797-2965
e-mail: ksommer@brook.edu
website: www.brookings.edu/es/urban/urban.htm
Researches metropolitan cooperation in the United States.

Citistates Group
650 Fairhaven Rd.
Fairhaven, MD 20779 USA
tel.: (301) 855-6482
e-mail: fpeters@citistates.com
website: www.citistates.com
These U.S. journalists write about metropolitan cooperation.

Danish Town Planning Institute
Peder Skrams Gade 2 B
DK-1054 Copenhagen K Denmark
tel.: 45 33 13 72 81; fax: 45 33 14 34 35

e-mail: dantown@inet.uni-c.dk
website: www.byplanlab.dk
Promotes urban and regional planning in Denmark.

European Academy of the Urban Environment
Bismarckallee 46-48
D-14193 Berlin, Germany
tel.: 49 30 89 59 99 0; fax: 49 30 89 59 99 19
e-mail: husch@eaue.de
website: www.eaue.de
Stimulates cooperation among European cities on environmental
issues.

Instituto de Pesquisa e Planejamento Urbano de Curitiba (IPPUC)
Rua Bom Jesus 669
Cabral, Curitiba, Paraná, Brasil CEP 80035-010
tel.: 55 41 352 1414; fax: 55 41 252 6679
e-mail: ippuc@ippuc.curitiba.pr.gov.br
website: www.ippuc.pr.gov.br
Researches sustainable urban development in Curitiba, Brazil.

Journal of World Transportation Policy and Practice
Le Frene, 8/10 rue Joseph Bara
F-75006 Paris, France
tel.: 33 01 4326 1323; tel/fax: 33 1 0 53 01 28 96
e-mail: postmaster@ecoplan.org
website: www.ecoplan.org/wtpp
Publishes articles on building more environmentally friendly
transportation systems.

Lincoln Institute of Land Policy
113 Brattle St.
Cambridge, MA 02138-3400 USA
tel.: (617) 661-3016 or (800) 526-3873
fax: (617) 661-7235 or (800) 526-3944
website: www.lincolninst.edu
Studies land use economics and taxation in the United States and
elsewhere.

Urban Land Institute
1025 Thomas Jefferson St., NW, Suite 500 West
Washington, DC 20007 USA
tel.: (202) 624-7000; fax: (202) 624-7140

e-mail: webmaster@uli.org
website: www.uli.org
Provides information and training to real estate developers.

Victoria Transport Policy Institute (VTPI)
1250 Rudlin St.
Victoria, BC, V8V 3R7 Canada
tel. and fax: (250) 360-1560
e-mail: info@vtpi.org
website: www.vtpi.org
Researches efficient and equitable transportation; keeps a list of
relevant studies.

Notes

1. Isaac Mburu, Nairobi resident, discussion with author, 19 February 2001; estimates relating to Nairobi population from Brian Williams, transport specialist, United Nations (U.N.) Centre for Human Settlements (Habitat), Nairobi, Kenya, discussion with author, 19 February 2001.

2. U.S. drivers from U.S. Department of Transportation (USDOT), Bureau of Transportation Statistics, *Transportation Statistics Annual Report 1997: Mobility and Access* (Washington, DC: USDOT Bureau of Transportation Statistics, 1997), p. 157; air pollution from Rita Seethaler, *Health Costs Due to Road Traffic-related Air Pollution: An Impact Assessment Project of Austria, France and Switzerland*, Synthesis Report, prepared for the World Health Organization (WHO) Ministerial Conference on Environment and Health, London, June 1999, p. 9, and from Nino Künzli et al., "Public-Health Impact of Outdoor and Traffic-Related Air Pollution: A European Assessment," *The Lancet*, 2 September 2000, pp. 795–801.

3. Obesity from Gary Taubes, "As Obesity Rates Rise, Experts Struggle to Explain Why," *Science*, 29 May 1998, pp. 1367–68; Lori Montgomery, "Suburbia's Road to Weight Gain: Land-Use Designs Discourage Pounding the Pavement, Some Say," *Washington Post*, 21 January 2001; transportation contribution to carbon emissions from International Energy Agency (IEA), CO_2 *Emissions from Fuel Combustion* (Paris: Organisation for Economic Co-operation and Development (OECD), 1999); carbon emissions contributing to climate change from J.T. Houghton et al., eds., *Climate Change 1995: The Science of Climate Change*, Contribution of Working Group I to the Second Assessment Report of the Intergovernmental Panel on Climate Change (Cambridge, U.K.: Cambridge University Press, 1996).

4. Atlanta from Tim Lomax et al., *2001 Urban Mobility Study* (College Station, TX: Texas Transportation Institute, 2001) on the Internet at <http://mobility.tamu.edu/2001/>; Bangkok from Richard Stren, "Transportation and Metropolitan Growth," in Richard Stren and Mila Freire, *The Challenge of Urban Government: Policies and Practices* (Washington, DC: World Bank Institute, 2001), p. 380; Jonathan D. Miller, *Emerging Trends in Real Estate* (New York: Lend Lease Real Estate Investments and PricewaterhouseCoopers LLP, October 2000).

5. Table 1 from U.N., Department of Economic and Social Affairs, Population Division, *World Urbanization Prospects: The 1999 Revision* (New York: 2000), Key Findings, <www.undp.org/popin/wdtrends/wdtrends. htm>, viewed 20 January 2001. Global urban population estimates are difficult to make, as the definition of "urban" and the reliability of census data vary from country to country. The U.N. figures cited here are for "urban agglomerations," which generally include the population in a city or town as well as that of adjacent suburbs.

6. Led by Peter Newman and Jeffrey Kenworthy, researchers at the

Institute for Sustainability and Technology Policy (ISTP) at Murdoch University in Perth, Australia, have done the most detailed surveys, measuring population density, transportation modal share, fuel use, and other indicators. Table 2 car use from Jeffrey R. Kenworthy and Felix B. Laube, with Peter W. G. Newman, Paul A. Barter, Tamim Raad, Chamlong Poboon, and Benedicto Guia, Jr., *An International Sourcebook of Automobile Dependence in Cities 1960–1990* (Boulder, CO: University Press of Colorado, 1999, p. 529; fuel use and population density from Peter Newman and Jeffrey Kenworthy, *Sustainability and Cities: Overcoming Automobile Dependence* (Washington, DC: Island Press, 1999), pp. 94–95, 70–71. Table 3 metropolitan area population estimates for 1995 from U.N., Department of Economic and Social Affairs, Population Division, *World Urbanization Prospects: The 1996 Revision* (New York: U.N., 1998), pp. 144–51; commute to work in Atlanta, Latin America, and Africa from Habitat, *Global Urban Indicators Database*, <www.urbanobservatory.org/indicators/database/transport.html>; commute to work in all other cities from Kenworthy and Laube et al., op. cit. this note, p. 529.

7.   Newman and Kenworthy, op. cit. note 6, pp. 112–13.

8.   L.J. Schipper, M.J. Figueroa, and R. Gorham, *People on the Move: A Comparison of Travel Patterns in OECD Countries*, Institute of Urban and Regional Development, University of California, Berkeley, cited in Lee Schipper and Celine Marie-Lilliu, *Transportation and CO$_2$ Emissions: Flexing the Link—A Path for the World Bank*, Environment Department Papers, Paper No. 69, September 1999, p. 57.

9.   Stephen B. Goddard, *Getting There: The Epic Struggle between Road and Rail in the American Century* (Chicago: University of Chicago Press, 1994).

10.   History from David Rusk, *Inside Game, Outside Game: Winning Strategies for Saving Urban America* (Washington, DC: Brookings Institution Press, 1999), pp. 91–92 ; highway miles in urban areas from USDOT, Federal Highway Administration (FHWA), Office of Highway Policy Information (OHPI), *Highway Statistics 1999*, <www.fhwa.dot.gov/ohim/hs99>, viewed 23 May 2001; highway spending by all levels of government from FHWA, OHPI, *Highway Statistics*, various years, and from FHWA, OHPI, *Highway Statistics Summary to 1995*, <www.fhwa.dot.gov/ohim/summary95>, viewed 23 May 2001; transit funding by all levels of government from American Public Transit Association, "Public Transportation Statistics," <www.apta.com/stats>, and from Terry Bronson, American Public Transit Association phone discussion with author, 25 May 2001.

11.   Highway financing from FHWA, "Financing Federal-Aid Highways," <www.fhwa.dot.gov/reports/fifahiwy>, viewed 23 May 2001; Atlanta from Margaret Pugh, *Moving Beyond Sprawl: The Challenge for Metropolitan Atlanta* (Washington, DC: Brookings Institution Center on Urban and Metropolitan Policy, 2000), p. 22.

12. Sewer investments from David K. Hamilton, *Governing Metropolitan Areas: Response to Growth and Change* (New York: Garland Publishing, 1999), pp. 151–52; Fannie Mae from Kenneth Jackson, *Crabgrass Frontier: The Suburbanization of the United States* (New York: Oxford University Press, 1985).

13. Jackson, op. cit. note 12.

14. U.S. Census data cited in Rusk, op. cit. note 10, pp. 68–69; gasoline from U.S. Department of Energy, Energy Information Administration, "World Apparent Consumption of Refined Petroleum Products, 1998," at <www.eia.doe.gov/pub/international/iea99/table35.xls>, viewed 29 May 2001.

15. Tamim Raad and Jeff Kenworthy, "The U.S. and Us," *Alternatives Journal*, vol. 24, no. 1, winter (1998), pp. 14–22.

16. Frances Frisken, L.S. Bourne, Gunter Gad, and Robert A. Murdie, "Governance and Social Sustainability: The Toronto Experience," in Mario Polèse and Richard Stren, *The Social Sustainability of Cities* (Toronto: The University of Toronto Press, 2000), pp. 68–97.

17. Difference in policies from Pietro S. Nivola, *Laws of the Landscape: How Policies Shape Cities in Europe and America* (Washington, DC: Brookings Institution Press, 1999). Table 4 from Tony Pattison, ed., *Jane's Urban Transport Systems 2000–2001* (London: Jane's Information Group, 2000), pp. 20–24.

18. Peep Mardiste et al., *Blueprints for Sustainable Transportation in Central and Eastern Europe* (Brussels: CEE Bankwatch Network, May 1997).

19. Peter S. Green, "Building Up Central Europe on a Western Base," *New York Times*, 16 May 2001; Czech Republic from Yaakov Garb, "Fighting Sprawl: Prague on the Edge," *Sustainable Transport*, fall 2000, p. 8, and from "Hypermarkets Coming on Strong in Czech Republic," *Discount Store News*, 7 February 2000.

20. Tim Burt, "Scope for Real Growth Is Likely in the Long Term," *Financial Times*, 14 June 2000.

21. Mario Lungo, "Urban Sprawl and Land Regulation in Latin America," *Land Lines*, Newsletter of the Lincoln Institute of Land Policy, March 2001, pp. 7–8; Christopher Zegras and Todd Litman, *An Analysis of the Full Costs and Impacts of Transportation in Santiago de Chile* (Washington, DC, and Santiago de Chile: International Institute for Energy Conservation, 1997) pp. 112–13.

22. Chinese subsidies from Hisashi Kubota and Tetsuo Kidokoro, "Analysis of Bicycle-Dependent Transport Systems in China: Case Study in a Medium-Sized City," *Transportation Research Record*, vol. 1441, 1994, pp. 11–15; dis-

couraging nonmotorized transport from John Whitelegg, "India's Roads to Ruin," *New Scientist*, 1 February 1997, p. 51, V. Setty Pendakur, "Urban Transportation in China: Trends and Issues," *Transportation Research Record*, vol. 1372, 1992, p. 7, and Henry T. Dimitriou, *A Developmental Approach to Urban Planning* (Aldershot, U.K.: Avebury, 1995); Surabaya from "A Breath of Fresh Air for Indonesia," *Sustainable Transport*, fall 2000, p. 17.

23. Habitat, *Reassessment of Urban Planning and Development Regulations in African Cities* (Nairobi: Habitat, 1999); Nairobi from R.A. Obudho, "Nairobi: National Capital and Regional Hub," in Carole Rakodi, ed., *The Urban Challenge in Africa* (Tokyo: U.N. University Press, 1997), and from Diana Lee-Smith and Davinder Lamba, "Social Transformation in a Post-colonial City: The Case of Nairobi," in Mario Polèse and Richard Stren, eds., *The Social Sustainability of Cities* (Toronto: University of Toronto Press, 2000).

24. Quote from USDOT, FHWA, *Our Nation's Travel: 1995 NPTS Early Results Report* (Washington, DC: FHWA, September 1997), p. 34; J. Solomon, *To Drive or Vote: Young Adults' Culture and Priorities* (London: Charter Institute of Transport, 1998) cited in John Adams, "The Social Implications of Hypermobility," Project on Environmentally Sustainable Transport: The Economic and Social Implications of Sustainable Transportation— Proceedings from the Ottawa Workshop (Paris: OECD, 1998).

25. U.S. population without driver's license from USDOT, op. cit. note 2, p. 182; children from USDOT, FHWA, op. cit. note 24, p. 29; women from FHWA, op. cit. this note, p. 16.

26. Atlanta Regional Commission, *Regional Transportation Plan Fact Book* (December 1998) p. 14, cited in Pugh, op. cit. note 11, p. 22; Bullard quoted in David Bollier, *How Smart Growth Can Stop Sprawl* (Washington, DC: Sprawl Watch Clearinghouse, 1998), p. 18.

27. Joel Hirschhorn, *Growing Pains: Quality of Life in the New Economy* (Washington, DC: National Governors Association, 2000); Myron Orfield, *Metropolitics: A Regional Agenda for Community and Stability* (Washington, DC, and Cambridge, MA: Brookings Institution Press and Lincoln Institute for Land Policy, 1997), pp. 9–10.

28. David Rusk, *Cities Without Suburbs* (Washington, DC: Woodrow Wilson Center Press, 1993), pp. 43–45; Manuel Pastor Jr., Peter Dreier, J. Eugene Grigsby III, Marta López-Garza, *Regions that Work: How Cities and Suburbs Can Grow Together* (Minneapolis: University of Minnesota Press, 2000), p. 99.

29. Lewis Mumford, *The City in History* (San Diego: Harcourt Brace, 1961), p. 507; Lomax et al., op. cit. note 4; Walter Hook, "Hurdles to Easing Congestion in Asia," *Habitat Debate* (Newsletter of U.N. Habitat), vol. 4, no. 2 (1998).

30. Marion Nestle and Michael F. Jacobson, "Halting the Obesity Epidemic:

A Public Health Policy Approach," *Public Health Reports*, January/February 2000, vol. 115, pp. 12–24.

31. Robert D. Putnam, *Bowling Alone* (New York: Simon and Schuster, 2000), pp. 204–15.

32. Jeff Kenworthy et al., *Indicators of Transport Efficiency in 37 Cities*, Report to the World Bank, 1997; Newman and Kenworthy, op. cit. note 6, pp. 123–24; Kenworthy et al., op. cit. note 6, pp. 619–20; Robert Cervero, *Efficient Urbanization: Economic Performance and the Shape of the Metropolis*, Lincoln Institute of Land Policy Working Paper (Cambridge, MA: 2000), p. 18.

33. Robert W. Burchell, "Costs and Benefits of Alternative Development Patterns: Sprawl Versus Smart Growth," in Lincoln Institute of Land Policy, *Metropolitan Development Patterns: Annual Roundtable 2000* (Cambridge, MA: 2000), pp. 47–49.

34. Surface Transportation Policy Project (STPP), *An Analysis of the Relationship Between Highway Expansion and Congestion in Metropolitan Areas: Lessons from the 15-year Texas Transportation Institute Study* (Washington, DC: 1998); Alan Sipress, "Widen the Roads, Drivers Will Come," *Washington Post*, 4 January 1999; Replogle quoted in David W. Chen, "The Cost of Urban Sprawl: Unplanned Obsolescence," *New York Times*, 30 January 2000.

35. Kenneth M. Gwilliam and Surhid Gautam, *Pollution from Motorcycles in Asia: Issues and Options*, World Bank Infrastructure Notes (Washington, DC: World Bank, April 2000); Peter Gaupp, "Air Pollution in the Third World," *Swiss Review of World Affairs*, February 1997; Utpal Chatterjee, "Expert Paints Gloomy Picture of Pollution," *Times of India*, 27 April 1998.

36. Ingredients in exhaust from Jack Hollander, ed., *The Energy-Environment Connection* (Washington, DC: Island Press, 1992); sulfur dioxide and particulate emissions records from U.N. Environment Programme (UNEP) and WHO, *Assessment of Urban Air Quality* (Nairobi: Global Environment Monitoring System (GEMS), 1998), daily particulate levels from Derek Elsom, *Smog Alert: Managing Urban Air Quality* (London: Earthscan, 1996); long-term exposure to particulates from WHO, "WHO Guidelines for Air Quality," Fact Sheet No. 187 (Geneva: December 1997) and from J. Raloff, "Clues Hint How Particulates Harm Lungs," *Science News*, 24 October 1998.

37. Anthony Faiola, "Santiago's Children Gasp for Cleaner Air," *Washington Post*, 12 July 1998; Atlanta from U.S. Environmental Protection Agency (EPA), "The Green Book: Nonattainment Areas for Criteria Pollutants," <www.epa.gov/oar/oaqps/greenbk>, viewed 24 May 2001; and from Georgia Department of Natural Resources, Environmental Protection Division, Air Protection Branch, "Ambient Monitoring Program," <uam.air.dnr.state.ga.us/amp/>, viewed 24 May 2001.

38. Traffic deaths from WHO, *The World Health Report 1995* (Geneva: 1995), and from Christopher Willoughby, *Managing Motorization*, Discussion Paper, Transport Division (Washington, DC: World Bank, April 2000), p. ii; cost from World Bank, "Roads and Highways Overview," <www.worldbank.org/ html/fpd/transport/roads_ss.htm>, viewed 7 June 2000; Newman and Kenworthy, op. cit. note 7.

39. Barbara McCann and Bianca DiLille, *Mean Streets 2000* (Washington, DC: STPP, June 2000).

40. Pedestrian deaths from ibid.; driver deaths and quote from Scott Bowles, "Elderly Die At A Record Pace Behind the Wheel," *USA Today*, 1 May 2001.

41. Figure 1 from IEA, op. cit. note 3. This figure shows values for carbon dioxide. Most Worldwatch publications show values only for the carbon content of the carbon dioxide gas (those numbers are smaller).

42. Walter Hook and Michael Replogle, "Motorization and Non-Motorized Transport in Asia," *Land Use Policy*, vol. 13, no. 1 (1996), pp. 69–84; Atlanta from Pugh, op. cit. note 11, and from Robert D. Bullard, Glenn S. Johnson, and Angel O. Torres, *Sprawl City: Race, Politics, and Planning in Atlanta* (Washington, DC: Island Press, 2000).

43. United States from Mark M. Glickman, "Beyond Gas Taxes: Linking Driving Fees to Externalities," (San Francisco: Redefining Progress, March 2001); FHWA, *Addendum to the 1997 Federal Highway Cost Allocation Study*, Final Report (Washington, DC: May 2000), on <www.fhwa.dot.gov/ policy/hcas/addendum.htm>, viewed 20 May 2001; Office of Technology Assessment, *Saving Energy in U.S. Transportation* (Washington, DC: U.S. Congress, Office of Technology Assessment, 1994); Todd Litman, "Transportation Cost Survey," (Victoria, BC: Victoria Transportation Policy Institute, 1992); James MacKenzie, Roger Dower, and Donald Chen, *The Going Rate: What It Really Costs to Drive* (Washington, DC: World Resources Institute, 1992); OECD, *Reforming Energy and Transport Subsidies: Environmental and Economic Implications* (Paris: 1997); James J. Murphy and Mark A. Delucchi, "A Review of the Literature on the Social Cost of Motor Vehicle Use in the United States," *Journal of Transportation and Statistics*, January 1998, pp. 14–42; Clifford Cobb, "The Roads Aren't Free," *Challenge*, May/June 1999; United Kingdom from David Maddison et al., *The True Costs of Road Transport* (London: Earthscan, 1996); international comparison from Christopher Willoughby, *Managing Motorization*, Discussion Paper, Transport Division (Washington, DC: World Bank, April 2000), p. ii; Santiago from Zegras and Litman, op. cit. note 21, and from Chris Zegras, "Clearing the Skies in Santiago," *Habitat Debate*, vol. 4, no. 2 (1998), pp. 23–25.

44. Jans Gehl and Lars Gemzøe, *Public Spaces Public Life: Copenhagen 1996* (Copenhagen: Arkitektens Forlag, Kunstakademiets Forlag, 1999), pp. 16–29, 40–43.

45. Robert Cervero, *The Transit Metropolis: A Global Inquiry* (Washington, DC: Island Press, 1998), pp. 132–54.

46. Gehl and Gemzøe, op. cit. note 44.

47. Cervero, op. cit. note 45.

48. Driving from Cervero, op. cit. note 45; reduction in energy use from Lynn Scholl, Lee Schipper, and Nancy Kiang, "CO_2 Emissions from Passenger Transport: A Comparison of International Trends from 1973 to 1992," *Energy Policy*, vol. 24, no. 1 (1996), p. 24; quote from public official cited in Gehl and Gemzøe, op. cit. note 44, p. 6.

49. Quote from Daniel Kennedy in "Safe Routes to School Story," <www.sustrans.org.uk>, viewed 6 May 2001.

50. Richard Moe and Carter Wilkie, *Changing Places* (New York: Henry Holt, 1997), pp. 211–34.

51. Jay Walljasper, "Portland's Green Peace: At Play In the Fields of Urban Planning," *The Nation*, 13 October 1997; view corridors from Moe and Wilkie, op. cit. note 50, p. 224.

52. Brad Berton, "Projects Preserve City's Architectural Heritage," *Business Journal-Portland*, 31 October 1997; William Thompson and John Hughel, "Back from the Brink," *Landscape Architecture*, July 1998, pp. 54–86.

53. Moe and Wilkie, op. cit. note 50, p. 229; 1000 Friends of Oregon, "Making the Connections: A Summary of the LUTRAQ Project," Volume 7, Integrating Land-Use and Transportation Planning for Livable Communities (Portland, OR: February 1997).

54. Metro plans from Metro, "Growth Management," <www.metro-region.org/growth/gms.html>, viewed 29 May 2001, and from Dan Mihalopoulos, "Two Ways to Control: Portland's Boundary Separates the Dream Homes from the Ducks," *St. Louis Post-Dispatch*, 26 February 1998; proximity to transit from Cervero, op. cit. note 45, pp. 416–23; light rail from Julian Wolinsky, "Light Rail: One Route to Livable Cities," *Railway Age*, July 1999, pp. 47–49.

55. Rusk, op. cit. note 10, pp. 165, 172–73.

56. Trade-offs from Peter Calthorpe and William Fulton, *The Regional City* (Washington, DC: Island Press, 2001), p. 115; Burton quoted in Rusk, op. cit. note 10, p. 177.

57. Pedestrian safety from McCann and DiLille, op. cit. note 39.

58. Steve Gutman, "CarSharing Portland: A Library With Cars Instead of

Books," *Orion Afield*, Autumn 2000, pp. 10–13.

59. Metro, "Regional Affordable Housing," <www.metro-region.org/growth/tfplan/affordable.html>, viewed 29 May 2001; Urban Land Institute, ULI Market Profiles 2000.

60. Arthur C. Nelson, "Regulations to Improve Development Patterns," in Lincoln Institute of Land Policy, op. cit. note 33, p. 78.

61. Curitiba history from Jonas Rabinovitch with Josef Leitman, Environmental Innovation and Management in Curitiba, Brazil, Urban Management Programme (UMP) Working Paper Series 1 (Washington, DC: UNDP/UNCHS/International Bank for Reconstruction and Development/ World Bank-UMP, 1993).

62. Bill McKibben, *Hope: Human and Wild* (Boston: Little, Brown and Company, 1995), pp 63–67.

63. Jonas Rabinovitch, "A Sustainable Urban Transportation System," *Energy for Sustainable Development* (Journal of the International Energy Initiative, July 1995, pp. 11–18; Figure 3 from Rabinovitch with Leitman, op. cit. note 61; zoning laws from Jonas Rabinovitch and John Hoehn, "A Sustainable Urban Transportation System: the "Surface Metro" in Curitiba, Brazil," report of the Environmental and Natural Resources Policy and Training Project (Madison, WI: University of Wisconsin, Madison, 19 May 1995), pp. 35–37.

64. Jonas Rabinovitch, "Innovative Land Use and Public Transport Policy," *Land Use Policy*, vol. 13, no. 1 (1996), pp. 51–67.

65. Rabinovitch, op. cit. note 64; Jonas Rabinovitch and Josef Leitman, "Urban Planning in Curitiba," *Scientific American*, March 1996, pp. 26–33; City Hall of Curitiba, International Relations Office, e-mail to author, 17 June 1998 (e-mail: sgm@pmc.curitiba.arauc.br).

66. Flood zoning from Rabinovitch with Leitman, op. cit. note 61, p. 26; City Hall of Curitiba, op. cit. note 65.

67. Rabinovitch with Leitman, op. cit. note 61; City Hall of Curitiba, op. cit. note 65.

68. Environmental education from Rabinovitch with Leitman, op. cit. note 61, pp. 44–47; children from McKibben, op. cit. note 62, pp. 86–89.

69. McKibben, op. cit. note 62, p. 61.

70. Deborah Lynn Bleviss, "Urban Transportation: Challenges Facing Latin America," (Washington, DC: InterAmerican Development Bank, 1999), <www.iadb.org/sds/doc/UrbanTransportBleviss.pdf>, p. 5.

71. Goddard, op. cit. note 9, p. 178.

72. Goddard, op. cit. note 9. Even the world's earliest cities had some form of planning to organize land use. In response to the Industrial Revolution, zoning was used in Western Europe to preserve the architectural character, light, and air of streets, and separate dirty industries from residences, but it developed furthest in the United States.

73. Yaakov Garb, Floersheimer Institute for Policy Studies, Jerusalem, Israel, phone interview, 1 May 2001; Yaakov Garb and Jonathan Levine, "How the Illusion of Strong Planning Undermines Planning: Anticipating the Trans-Israel Highway's Land-Use Impacts," draft manuscript distributed to accompany presentation at the conference on "Fifty Years of Planning in Israel: Theory and Practice," *Technion*, December 1998.

74. Lloyd Wright, U.S. Agency for International Development, presentation at United Nations Commission on Sustainable Development, New York, 18 May 2001.

75. Studies from VNG uitgeverij, *The Economic Significance of Cycling: A Study to Illustrate the Costs and Benefits of Cycling Policy* (The Hague: 2000); *woonerf* from Spiro Kostof, *The City Assembled* (Boston: Bullfinch Press/Little Brown and Company, 1992), pp. 240–41.

76. European Commission, *European Sustainable Cities* (Brussels: 1996); Germany from "They Couldn't Car Less," *Grist Magazine*, 10 March 2000; Car Free Cities Network on the Internet at <www.eurocities.org/networks/netprog.html>, viewed 4 February 1999.

77. Oscar Edmundo Diaz, "Awake at the Wheel: Bogotá's Response to the Transportation Challenge," *Encompass*, vol. 5, no. 3 (February/March 2001), pp. 5–7; Enrique Peñalosa, visiting scholar at New York University, New York, discussion with author, 3 May 2001; Steven Ambrus, "Bogotá Takes a Breather," *EcoAmericas*, March 2000, p. 10.

78. Haynes C. Goddard, "Using Tradeable Permits to Achieve Sustainability in the World's Largest Cities," *Environmental and Resource Economics*, July 1997, pp. 63–99, and from Gunnar S. Eskeland and Shantayanan Devarajan, *Taxing Bads by Taxing Goods: Pollution Control with Presumptive Charges* (Washington, DC: World Bank, 1996).

79. Diaz, op. cit. note 77; Jimmy Weiskopf, "Bogotá Among First Latin American Capitals to Implement Day Restricting Use of Cars," *International Environment Reporter*, 15 March 2000, pp. 148–49.

80. Robert Cervero, "Paratransit: The Gap Fillers," *Habitat Debate*, vol. 4, no. 2 (1998), pp. 8–9.

81. PIARC Committee on Intelligent Transport, "Fighting Traffic with

Technology," *The Futurist*, September–October 2000, p. 30; personal rapid transit from University of Washington, "Personal Rapid Transit (PRT) Quicklinks," <faculty.washington.edu/~jbs/itrans/prtquick.htm>, viewed 1 June 2001, and from University of Bristol, Advanced Transport Group, "Transport for the Future," <atg.fen.bris.ac.uk/ultra.html>, viewed 1 June 2001.

82. Kenworthy et al., op. cit. note 6, pp. 547–50.

83. Quote from Emin Tengström, *Towards Environmental Sustainability? A Comparative Study of Danish, Dutch and Swedish Transport Policies in a European Context* (Aldershot, U.K.: Ashgate Publishing, 1999), pp. 77–85; "ABC" policy from Gary Haq, *Towards Sustainable Transport Planning: A Comparison between Britain and the Netherlands* (Aldershot, U.K.: Avebury Publishing, 1997), p. 99.

84. "Bangkok's Train, Running on Empty," *The Economist*, 23 December 2000, p. 46.

85. Congress for the New Urbanism, *Charter of the New Urbanism* (New York: McGraw Hill, 2000); Andres Dvany, Elizabeth Plater-Zyberk, and Jeff Speck, *Suburban Nation: The Rise of Sprawl and the Decline of the American Dream* (New York: Farrar, Straus and Giroux, 2000).

86. Historical ratio from Arnulf Grübler, *The Rise and Fall of Infrastructures: Dynamics of Evolution and Technological Change in Transport* (New York: Springer-Verlag, 1990), pp. 254–58; past expectations from Frank W. Geels and Wim A. Smit, "Failed Technology Futures: Pitfalls and Lessons From A Historical Survey," *Futures*, vol. 32 (2000), pp. 867–85.

87. Joel Kotkin, *The New Geography: How the Digital Revolution Is Reshaping the American Landscape* (New York: Random House, 2000), p. 7; Peter Hall, *Cities in Civilization* (New York: Pantheon Books, 1998), p. 963.

88. State of Maryland Smart Growth Program, <www.op.state.md.us/smartgrowth/smartwhat.htm>, viewed 4 January 2001; Lori Montgomery, "Md. Going 'Beyond the Pavement'; State Shifting Focus From Roads to Pedestrians," *Washington Post*, 15 September 2000; Edward T. McMahon, "Why Can't Johnny Walk to School?" Elm Street Writers Group, <www.mlui.org/projects/growthmanagement/elmstreet/mcmahon.html>, viewed 12 April 2001.

89. Estimates from Garb, op. cit. note 73. A recent survey of 70 U.S. cities found that, on average, 15 percent of developable urban land was vacant, ranging from undisturbed open space to previously used "brownfields." Michael A. Pagano and Ann O'M. Bowman, "Vacant Land in Cities: An Urban Resource," (Washington, DC: Brookings Institution Center on Urban and Metropolitan Policy Survey Series, December 2000).

90. Joel S. Hirschhorn, *New Mission for Brownfields: Attacking Sprawl By*

Revitalizing Older Communities (Washington, DC: National Governors Association, 2000), p. 8.

91. Garb, op. cit. note 73.

92. Paul S. Grogan and Tony Proscio, *Comeback Cities: A Blueprint for Urban Neighborhood Revival* (Boulder, CO: Westview Press, 2000), pp. 103–26.

93. David B. Goldstein, "Making Housing More Affordable: Correcting Misplaced Incentives in the Lending System," (San Francisco: Natural Resources Defense Council, May 1996); Congress for the New Urbanism, op. cit. note 85, Location Efficient Mortgage, <http://locationefficiency.com>, viewed 11 April 2001.

94. David Perry, ed., *Building the Public City: The Politics, Governance, and Finance of Public Infrastructure* (Thousand Oaks, CA: Sage Publications, 1995); Roy Bahl and Johannes Linn, *Urban Public Finance in Developing Countries* (New York: Oxford University Press for the International Bank for Reconstruction and Development, 1992); Kenneth C. Wenzer, ed., *Land-Value Taxation: The Equitable and Efficient Source of Public Finance* (Armonk, NY: M.E. Sharpe, 1999).

95. Kenya from VNG uitgeverij, op. cit. note 75, p. 42; Lima from Paul Guitink, Senior Transportation Specialist, World Bank, Washington, DC, discussion with author, 4 May 2001.

96. Jos Dings, Centre for Energy Conservation and Environmental Technology, Delft, Netherlands, discussion with author 22 February 2001; variable costs from Todd Litman, *The Costs of Automobile Dependency* (Victoria, BC, Canada: Victoria Transport Policy Institute, 1996); Figure 3 from American Automobile Association, *Your Driving Costs*, 1998 ed., cited in Stacy C. Davis, *Transportation Energy Data Book: Edition 19* (Oak Ridge, TN: Oak Ridge National Laboratory, September 1999), pp. 5-14–5-15.

97. Table 6 contains national average prices and taxes for most countries from International Energy Agency (IEA), *Monthly Price Statistics: End-User Oil Product Prices and Average Crude Oil Import Costs*, October 2000, <www.iea.org/statist/index.htm>, viewed 2 December 2000; for Brazil, India, South Africa, China, Russia, and Indonesia, capital city prices and $.32 untaxed world average price are from Gerhard Metschies, *GTZ Fuel Price Survey 2000* (Eschborn, Germany: Deutsche Gesellschaft für Technische Zusammenarbeit (GTZ), forthcoming), with preliminary data from idem, GTZ, e-mail to author, 28 December 2000. Price adjustments from Gerhard P. Metschies, *Fuel Prices and Taxation: With Comparative Tables for 160 Countries* (Eschborn, Germany: GTZ, May 1999).

98. Per Kågeson and Jos Dings, *Electronic Kilometre Charging for Heavy Goods Vehicles in Europe* (Brussels: European Federation for Transport and Environment, 1999).

99. Pricing from H. William Batt, "Motor Vehicle Transportation and Proper Pricing: User Fees, Environmental Fees, and Value Capture," *Ecological Economics Bulletin*, First Quarter 1998, pp. 10–14; Singapore from David Weller, "For Whom the Road Tolls: Road Pricing in Singapore," *Harvard International Review*, summer 1998, pp. 10–11, and from Charles P. Wallace, "Singapore's Attempt to Curb Traffic," *San Francisco Chronicle*, 7 February 1995.

100. Federal laws from Donald C. Shoup, "An Opportunity to Reduce Minimum Parking Requirements," *APA Journal*, winter 1995, and from Office of Senator Lincoln Chafee, U.S. Congress, "Chafee Touts New 'Commuter Choice', Employee Benefits," *Capitol Hill Press Releases*, 8 December 1998; Maryland from Michael Replogle and Lisa Swann, "A Pay Raise for Not Driving to Work," press release (Washington, DC: Environmental Defense, 11 May 2000).

101. Chris Kavalec and James Woods, "Towards Marginal Cost Pricing of Accident Risk: The Energy, Travel and Welfare Impacts of Pay-at-the-Pump Auto Insurance," *Energy Policy*, vol. 27 (1999), pp. 331–42; Todd Litman, "Distance-based Vehicle Insurance as a TDM Strategy," *Transportation Quarterly*, vol. 51, no. 3 (1997), pp. 119–137.

102. Mardiste et al., op. cit. note 18.

103. Robert Puentes, *Flexible Funding for Transit: Who Uses It?* (Washington, DC: Brookings Institution Center on Urban and Metropolitan Policy, May 2000); STPP, *Changing Direction: Federal Transportation Spending in the 1990s* (Washington, DC: March 2000), p. 20; Don Chen, STPP, Washington, DC, discussion with author, 30 August 2000.

104. Quote from Federal Housing Administration 1938 "Underwriting Manual" from Evan McKenzie, *Privatopia: Homeowner Associations and the Rise of Residential Private Government* (New Haven: Yale University Press, 1994), pp. 64–65.

105. Mike Burton quoted in Molly O'Meara, "How Mid-Sized Cities Can Avoid Strangulation," *World Watch*, September/October 1998, p. 13.

106. Raad and Kenworthy, op. cit. note 15, pp. 15–16.

107. Frisken et al., op. cit. note 16; Raad and Kenworthy, op. cit. note 15, p. 18.

108. Raad and Kenworthy, op. cit. note 15, p. 18; Joe Chidley, "The Fight for Toronto: A Proposed Merger Draws Cries of Outrage from Rich and Poor, Right and Left," *MacLean's*, 17 March 1997; Richard Brennan, "Province Fights Traffic Gridlock With $250 Million for Transit," *Toronto Star*, 10 May 2001.

109. Andrew Reschovsky, "The Impact of Decentralization on Cities' Fiscal Health: Lessons from the United States," in Shahid Yusuf, Weiping Wu, and Simon Evenett, eds., *Local Dynamics in an Era of Globalization* (Washington, DC: World Bank, 2000), pp. 148–58.

110. France from Reschovsky, op. cit. note 109.

111. Report on the U.N. International Roundtable on Transportation Energy Efficiency and Sustainable Development, 5–7 December 1999, Cairo, Egypt; "World Bank Lending for Transport," <www.worldbank.org/html/fpd/transport/lending.htm>, viewed 7 June 2000; Magda Stoczkiewicz, "The Conditions Attached to Western Money," *T&E Bulletin* (newsletter of the European Federation for Transport and Environment, Brussels), May 2000; Magda Stoczkiewicz, Central and Eastern Europe (CEE) Bankwatch Network, Brussels, discussion with author, 2 October 2000.

112. Mumford, op. cit. note 29, p. 486.

113. Alex Marshall, *How Cities Work* (Austin: University of Texas Press, 2000), p. 193 and 195.

114. Anton Nelessen quoted in Ruth Eckdish Knack, "Tony Nelessen's Do-It-Yourself Neotraditionalism," *Planning*, vol. 57, no. 12 (December 1991), p. 18; Calthorpe and Fulton, op. cit. note 56.

115. Calthorpe and Fulton, op. cit. note 56, pp. 128–38.

116. Ted Turner quoted in Sue Anne Presley, "Atlanta's Booming Growth Is No Easy Ride," *Washington Post*, 4 December 1998; anti-sprawl platform from Jill Jordan Sieder, "Traffic Jam: In Atlanta, A Pitched Battle Over Roads, Pollution, and Boundless Urban Sprawl," *U.S. News & World Report*, 8 February 1999, p. 28; new agency from Russ Bynum, "Ga. Lawmakers OK Anti-Sprawl Agency," *Associated Press*, 25 March 1999.

117. Patricio Lanfranco, Ciudad Viva, Santiago de Chile, discussion with author, 18 April 2001.

118. Jessica Alexander, "Ciclistas Furiosos Pedal in Protest," *Christian Science Monitor*, 16 August 2000; John Roach, "Cyclists Plug Santiago Streets to Protest Smog," *Environmental News Network*, 2 October 2000; Lanfranco, op. cit. note 117.

119. Jeffrey Maganya, Program Manager for the Transport Program in East Africa, Intermediate Technology Development Group (ITDG), Nairobi, Kenya, discussion with author, 8 May 2001.

120. Guitink, op. cit. note 95.

121. Frazer Goodwin, Policy Officer, European Federation for Transport and

Environment, Brussels, phone discussion with author, 21 September 2000; Western European governments shifting taxes from David Malin Roodman, "Environmental Tax Shifts Multiplying," in Lester R. Brown et al., *Vital Signs 2000: The Environmental Trends That Are Shaping Our Future* (New York: W.W. Norton & Company, 2000), pp. 138–139.

122. Klaas Breunissen, Milieudefensie, Amsterdam, Netherlands, discussion with author, 3 April 2001.

123. Lynn Sloman, Assistant Director, Transport 2000, London, United Kingdom, discussion with author, 10 October 2000.

124. Maganya, op. cit. note 119.

125. Lloyd Wright, U.S. Agency for International Development, presentation at the U.N. Commission on Sustainable Development, 18 April 2001; 38 states from Hirschhorn, op. cit. note 27, p. 64; 1000 Friends from Donald C. Williams, *Urban Sprawl: A Reference Handbook* (Santa Barbara, CA: ABC-CLIO, 2000), pp. 170–172; elections and ballot initiatives from Phyllis Myers and Robert Puentes, *Growth at the Ballot Box: Electing the Shape of Communities in November 2000* (Washington, DC: Brookings Institution, February 2001).

126. Psychology from Keith Bradsher, "Was Freud a Minivan or S.U.V. Kind of Guy?" *New York Times*, 17 July 2000; Table 7 from "Total Measured U.S. Ad Spending by Category & Media in 1998" and "Measured Ad Spending by Category," *Advertising Age*, <http://adage.com/dataplace/archives/dp409.html>, viewed 19 July 2000; Anna Wilde Mathews, "Ford Motor Gets Starring Role on WB Network," *Wall Street Journal*, 21 March 2001.

127. Garb, op. cit. note 19, p. 9; Walter Hook, Executive Director, Institute for Transportation and Development Policy, New York, discussion with author, 28 September 2000.

128. Fred S. McChesney, *Money for Nothing: Politicians, Rent Extraction, and Political Extortion* (Cambridge, MA: Harvard University Press, 1997); Holly Bailey, "The Big Winners: A Look at Tax Breaks Won by Special Interests," *Money in Politics Alert,* Center for Responsive Politics, Washington, DC, 2 August 1999; contributions of real estate, construction, transportation, and oil and gas industries from Center for Responsive Politics, "2000 Election Overview," <www.opensecrets.org/2000elect/storysofar/sectors.asp>, viewed 25 May 2001; J.L. Laws, "Boehlert Seeks Bipartisan Bloc to Fight CAFE Rider," *Energy and Environment Daily*, 13 March 2000, pp. 11–12.

129. European Commission, *Transport in Figures*, <www.europa.eu.int>, viewed 29 January 2001; U.S. from American Public Transit Association (APTA), "For Fifth Straight Year, Public Transportation on the Rise," press release (Washington, DC: 16 April 2001).

130. Europe from <www.carsharing.net>, viewed 16 May 2001, and from Mary Williams Walsh, "Car Sharing Holds the Road in Germany," *Los Angeles Times*, 23 July 1998; U.S. from Fred Bayles, "A Hot Import: Communal Cars for Congested Streets," *USA Today*, 21 July 2000; William Clay Ford, Jr., Speech at the 5th Annual Greenpeace Business Conference, London, 5 October 2000.

131. E.B. White, *One Man's Meat* (New York: Harper & Row, 1944); Congress of the New Urbanism, <www.cnu.org>, viewed 16 May 2001.

132. Lanfranco, op. cit. note 117.

133. Stoczkiewicz, discussion with author, op. cit. note 111; Garb, op. cit. note 73.

134. Goddard, op. cit. note 9, p. 114.

135. Enrique Peñalosa, former mayor of Bogotá, presentation at the United Nations, New York, 18 April 2001; Bremen Initiative, "New Partnerships for the 21st Century," <www.bremen-initiative.de/news/>, viewed 25 May 2001.

136. U.K. from Maddison et al., op. cit. note 43, p. 6; U.S. from Pew Center for Civic Journalism, *Straight Talk from Americans-2000*, Survey conducted by Princeton Survey Research Associates for the Pew Center for Civic Journalism, February 2000; Haya El Nasser, "Survey Favors Controlling Sprawl," *USA Today*, 17 October 2000.

137. Eisenhower quoted in Goddard, op. cit. note 9, p. 194.

138. Peñalosa, op. cit. note 135.

Worldwatch Papers

No. of Copies

Worldwatch Papers by Molly O'Meara Sheehan

_____WWP0156 City Limits: Putting the Brakes on Sprawl

_____WWP0147 Reinventing Cities for People and the Planet

Climate Change, Energy, and Materials

_____WWP0151 Micropower: The Next Electrical Era

_____WWP0149 Paper Cuts: Recovering the Paper Landscape

_____WWP0144 Mind Over Matter: Recasting the Role of Materials in Our Lives

_____WWP0138 Rising Sun, Gathering Winds: Policies to Stabilize the Climate and Strengthen Economies

_____WWP0130 Climate of Hope: New Strategies for Stabilizing the World's Atmosphere

_____WWP0124 A Building Revolution: How Ecology and Health Concerns Are Transforming Construction

Ecological and Human Health

_____WWP0153 Why Poison Ourselves? A Precautionary Approach to Synthetic Chemicals

_____WWP0148 Nature's Cornucopia: Our Stake in Plant Diversity

_____WWP0145 Safeguarding The Health of Oceans

_____WWP0142 Rocking the Boat: Conserving Fisheries and Protecting Jobs

_____WWP0141 Losing Strands in the Web of Life: Vertebrate Declines and the Conservation of Biological Diversity

_____WWP0140 Taking a Stand: Cultivating a New Relationship with the World's Forests

_____WWP0129 Infecting Ourselves: How Environmental and Social Disruptions Trigger Disease

_____WWP0128 Imperiled Waters, Impoverished Future: The Decline of Freshwater Ecosystems

Economics, Institutions, and Security

_____WWP0155 Still Waiting for the Jubilee: Pragmatic Solutions for the Third World Debt Crisis

_____WWP0152 Working for the Environment: A Growing Source of Jobs

_____WWP0146 Ending Violent Conflict

_____WWP0139 Investing in the Future: Harnessing Private Capital Flows for Environmentally Sustainable Development

_____WWP0137 Small Arms, Big Impact: The Next Challenge of Disarmament

_____WWP0134 Getting the Signals Right: Tax Reform to Protect the Environment and the Economy

_____WWP0133 Paying the Piper: Subsidies, Politics, and the Environment

_____WWP0127 Eco-Justice: Linking Human Rights and the Environment

_____WWP0126 Partnership for the Planet: An Environmental Agenda for the United Nations

_____WWP0125 The Hour of Departure: Forces That Create Refugees and Migrants

_____WWP0122 Budgeting for Disarmament: The Costs of War and Peace

Food, Water, Population, and Urbanization

_____WWP0150 Underfed and Overfed: The Global Epidemic of Malnutrition

_____WWP0143 Beyond Malthus: Sixteen Dimensions of the Population Problem

_____WWP0136 The Agricultural Link: How Environmental Deterioration Could Disrupt Economic Progress

_____WWP0135 Recycling Organic Waste: From Urban Pollutant to Farm Resource

_____WWP0132 Dividing the Waters: Food Security, Ecosystem Health, and the New Politics of Scarcity

_____WWP0131 Shrinking Fields: Cropland Loss in a World of Eight Billion

_____Total copies (transfer number to order form on next page)

PUBLICATION ORDER FORM

NOTE: Many Worldwatch publications can be downloaded as PDF files from our website at **www.worldwatch.org**. Orders for printed publications can also be placed on the web.

_____ *State of the World:* **$15.95**
The annual book used by journalists, activists, scholars, and policymakers worldwide to get a clear picture of the environmental problems we face.

_____ **State of the World Library: $30.00 (international subscribers $45)**
Receive *State of the World* and all Worldwatch Papers as they are released during the calendar year.

_____ *Vital Signs:* **$13.95**
The book of trends that are shaping our future in easy-to-read graph and table format, with a brief commentary on each trend.

_____ **WORLD WATCH magazine subscription: $20.00 (international subscribers $35.00)**
Stay abreast of global environmental trends and issues with our award-winning, eminently readable bimonthly magazine.

_____ **Worldwatch CD-ROM: $99.00**
Contains global agricultural, energy, economic, environmental, social, and military indicators from all current Worldwatch publications. Includes *Vital Signs* and *State of the World* as they are published. CD contains Microsoft Excel spreadsheets 5.0/95 (*.xls) for Windows, and works on both Mac and PC.

_____ **Worldwatch Papers—See list on previous page Single copy: $5.00**
any combination of titles: 2–5: $4.00 ea. • 6–20: $3.00 ea. • 21 or more: $2.00 ea.

$4.00* Shipping and Handling *($8.00 outside North America)*
minimum charge for S&H; call (800) 555-2028 for bulk order S&H

_____ **TOTAL** (U.S. dollars only)

Make check payable to: Worldwatch Institute, P.O. Box 879 Oxon Hill, MD 20797 USA

❑ Enclosed is my check or purchase order for U.S. $_____

❑ AMEX ❑ VISA ❑ MasterCard _____
                            Card Number   Expiration Date

signature

name   **daytime phone #**

address

city   **state**   **zip/country**

phone: (800) 555-2028   fax: (301) 567-9553   e-mail: wwpub@worldwatch.org
website: www.worldwatch.org

Wish to make a tax-deductible contribution? Contact Worldwatch to find out how your donation can help advance our work.